HUMANITY'S EPIC AWAKENING

A Mystical Odyssey Beyond Belief

Mary Reed
Featuring poetry by Chelan Harkin

This book is available on Amazon.
ISBN: 9798377209492

Cover art and production by Cheri Warren.
Interior art by Ashlee Eikelboom.
Formatting by Isabell VanMerlin.

This book is dedicated to my private community.
I am honored to be on this adventure with you.

Chelan Harkin's poetry is featured throughout this book because her voice confirms and lifts my own. Our words differ but the same Divine force inspires us to speak. While four of Chelan's poems are here in their entirety, the poetry between chapters are snippets from various works in her impressive, ever-expanding collection.

The sun and the bud
have the same yearning
to bring the inner essence
of the rose forward.

CONTENTS

INTRODUCTION

Given the hectic pace of our rapidly changing world, it would be nice to think of humanity's spiritual awakening as something akin to following a well-lit path out of a frenetic urban landscape and into a peaceful meadow of tulips. But alas, that is not what is happening; our awakening is more of a bull-in-china-shop kind of experience. However, as you will see in this book, we are already much further along in our awakening than most people realize, and we are fast approaching the point where we will be able to let that bull go frolic in the tulips while we start having fun with our newly-remembered ability to create universes.

Before we explore the full trajectory of our fascinating journey, I must address two issues that risk distracting readers. First, I use a range of labels to refer to the Almighty Being. You will see common terms such as God, Source, Creator, Oneness, Divine Love, and Monad, any of which may have historical associations that dilute or pollute relationship to the subject. Regardless of any discomfort or prejudice readers may have with these terms, in truth no label I use will come close to conveying the full visceral *experience* of The Big It. I experience God simply as All There Is, beyond intellectual understanding and beyond the limitations of words. I recommend readers simply lean into the feeling of what is written, for truth always recognizes the feeling of truth.

The second potential distraction is curiosity about who I am to write this text. In my first book, *Unwitting Mystic: Evolution of the Message of Love,* I detailed how my

1

unexpected spiritual awakening started in 2000 when I was a staunchly agnostic healthcare executive and inexplicably began having uncontrollable metaphysical experiences. Since then I have had countless mystical engagements in otherworldly Divine realms, often involving Jesus (likely because I knew him in my heart as a child) as well as other Christian, Buddhist, Hindu, and unaffiliated entities.

These mystical events can occur at any time: while I am simply going about my day, in meditation, in the semi-alert states going to or coming out of sleep, and on rare occasion under hypnosis. I have never done drugs, so none of my experiences have been induced by hallucinogens such as ayahuasca or MDMA. In *Unwitting Mystic* I shared the shock and disorientation that came with having the ability to connect with Divine realms and beings, and I explained the circumstances under which each experience happened. I brought readers along on my personal journey from a "normal" life in Washington, DC to a monastic life in a Buddhist nunnery in the Himalayas, sharing the ecstasy, the confusion, the devastation that led to a suicide attempt, and my eventual self acceptance.

I will not share that level of personal detail in this text. This is not about my personal journey. This is about *our* journey. While I include herein several events previously mentioned in *Unwitting Mystic* and in my second book, *Divine New Being*, every experience chosen for this text serves solely as a building block to understanding the bigger picture of humanity's evolution through my own embodied experiences of it. My intention in narrating our story using the as-they-happened details of my events is to convey both the wisdom inherent in them and the broader context to which the wisdom pertains. I will include supplemental personal information only when it aids in content or context.

While this book is not about the personal story of who I am, it is, in fact, an illumination of *what* I am. On December 17, 2000, I traveled backwards through a tunnel of light at incredible speed, continuing on and on until I found myself as a point of awareness suspended deep in the cosmos among the stars. With a reverberation so powerful it was as though the cosmos itself was speaking, I said, "I am The Message." I looked down at planet Earth and continued, "I am to be revealed in this world as The Message." I watched my entry into Earth then; it appeared like a pinprick on the earth's surface, entirely unnoticed, insignificant, and anonymous. Concentric circles of energy slowly began to radiate out from where I entered and eventually encircled the planet.

Notice in this experience I did not say, "I am The Messenger." I am not here to give a message. I am here to *be* The Message. I am a harbinger of humanity's awakening, embodying a Divine perspective of where we have been, where we are now, and what we are waking up into. As I share with others the truth of my experiences and the Divine wisdom I glean therein, I reveal, and in a way transmit, the energy of remembrance and recognition. And I am not the only one doing this. There are many others like me emerging throughout humanity, each of us gleaning Divine wisdom in myriad ways through our unique lenses and angles of perception. As we share our experiences with others, we catalyze change and increase the momentum of awakening for individuals and the collective.

The hallmark of the transformation at hand is direct-with-Source experiences that allow us to transcend old beliefs we have been taught through societal, cultural, and religious conditioning. We are beginning now to embody or connect *directly* with Divine wisdom and understanding to realize fundamental truths about ourselves, reality, and God. In *Divine New Being* I describe what happens in my own metaphysical experiences as being similar to encountering a blackboard with spiritual lessons written on it, but instead of looking at the lessons to learn them, I enter into the blackboard and become the lessons themselves. The experiences are not mental at all; they are not an act of believing or studying information to try to understand. They are the embodiment of the information itself. There are millions of documented cases of people who have had similar embodied events through near-death experiences (NDEs) that allowed them to directly realize astounding wisdom on "the other side." (The International Association for Near-Death Studies reports up to 15% of the population has had NDEs.) But in our awakening world, more and more people are coming into these transformative experiences in ways that don't require such severe life-threatening impact on the physical body.

These direct-with-Source experiences continue to increase throughout humanity as the momentum of our spiritual awakening accelerates because what we are waking up into is the remembrance of *what* we really are — indeed what all life is — which is God itself in expression. We embody the knowing, the living truth, that we have never been separate from God. The very words you read in this moment are of God, as are the eyes that read them, the hands that wrote them, and the book or device conveying them. Supplier, supply, and supplied to: God, God, and God.

Chelan Harkin, the quintessential mystic poet of our day who is featured in this text, captures this shift in understanding eloquently in these stanzas from her poem, The Worst Thing:

The worst thing we ever did
was put God in the sky
out of reach
pulling divinity from the leaf
sifting out the holy from our bones,
insisting God isn't bursting dazzlement
through everything we've made
a hard commitment to see as ordinary,
stripping the sacred from everywhere
to put in a cloud man elsewhere
prying closeness from our heart.

The worst thing we ever did was pretend
God isn't the easiest thing
in this Universe
available to every soul
in every breath.

In her book *Oneness,* the author Rasha articulates this shift in understanding even more overtly: *The inclination to place the concept of God in an exalted position within the framework of a personal philosophy is at the root of all that holds one back in one's experience of God. For God is not within you to be worshipped, or feared, or even to be understood, but rather, to be experienced and known. The very act of the exultation of the Divine creates a delineation between that Divine presence and oneself — a state of separation that constitutes a barrier to the very connection that one most fervently wishes to realize. The God within all life does not seek to be placed on a pedestal, but hopes to be discovered as the source of one's own essence.*

The process for realizing the truth of our Oneness — our innate with-and-of-God truth — requires that we work compassionately with the human mind that has for eons been powerfully conditioned through fear to believe that we are separate from God and all "other" in life. When we understand that our collective consciousness, or humanity's overall mindset, has been oriented in this belief in separation from God, we begin to realize the incredible burden of fear our precious minds have carried in feeling alone and responsible for figuring out how make it on our own. Alfred K. LaMotte, an American professor of World Religions and an interfaith chaplain, gently referred to the compassionate evolution from separation consciousness to Oneness realization when he wrote: *"Christ" is the vibration of pure Love emanating from awakened Silence inside us. "Christos" means "Anointed One." First, we meet the Christos as an other (as in Jesus), though the Christos is our own deepest Self. The Beloved's energy sustains us until we are ready to anoint ourselves.*

We are ready, and have already begun, to anoint ourselves. The separate self is ready and has begun realizing the Christed Self.

The days of denying our ability to directly connect to our own innate truth are coming to an end. Humanity has collectively chosen to transcend the fearful mindset that conditioned us to believe we are separate from God. In fact, remembrance of our unity with and in God has already occurred, as I and others demonstrate through our experiences. But most people are not yet aware of this remembrance — this resurrection, if you will — because in the same way the light of a new star takes many years to reach our perception, so too does the light of Divine realization. Paul Selig, who channels an astonishing volume of information on our collective awakening, writes about this time of transcending fear-based living in his book *Resurrection: The true sense of self, the one who knows who he is, what he is, and how he serves, has already risen above fear. And re-articulation, or resurrection, embodiment, manifestation as the Monad, aligns you beyond fear. It simply does not express at the level of vibration you are coming to.*

It is worth noting here that Paul Selig's work confirms what Alfred K. LaMotte wrote about being sustained by "others" until we realize our own Divine truth. When Selig was asked who the guides are that he channels, he said, "While they have given a name, that is just a symbol. The guides say that, in fact, they are who you become when you know who you really are." This is my own experience of guides as well. I have needed all manner of "others" to help guide me until I was ready to truly realize myself as the Divine in expression.

The light of Divine realization is dawning on people all around the world now; we recognize it when we begin to literally feel like we're waking up from a soul-level sleep. As each individual allows that light into their being, it seeps evermore into the collective consciousness. And that exquisitely loving light is starting to fracture all manner of darkness in our fear-based world, causing all manner of confusion and mayhem. You may have noticed that there is no such thing as conventional "normal" anymore. The foundations of old paradigms that dictated how we are expected to conform to oppressive limiting standards of being human are collapsing. Feeling a hint of newfound freedom, we find ourselves now seeking to align deeply with our own truth. We are demanding resonance with that which feels profoundly right in both our soul and our bones. We want to know, experience, and live freely in our innate Divine truth.

Until living in that Divine truth becomes the norm and we are fully aware of the light of the Divine here as us, the confusion and mayhem will continue. This chaotic process of breaking down and releasing the constricting limitations of old is not unlike the way the acorn cracks open to know itself as the oak tree and the caterpillar completely transforms itself to take flight as the butterfly. The confining form of old must be released to allow our full potential to express.

This book reveals much of what our greater potential holds for us. The views of evolution I offer come from inside our collective reunion with and in God as I have experienced it numerous times in Divine realms and in the company of Divine beings. Together these events provide sage understanding of where humanity has been, where we are now, and what we are waking up into. As we venture into that entire trajectory now, you will see why, from the mystical vantage point, our awakening is truly an epic and wildly inspiring odyssey.

PART ONE

WHERE WE HAVE BEEN

IT IS FINALLY HEALED

*The sign that
it is finally
healed*

*is when a wound
is alchemized
into a story*

*that dresses
the wound
of another.*

ONE

THE ORIGINAL THOUGHT

Humanity's awakening is both an exciting creative momentum and an inevitably destructive one. But before we can step confidently into our full creative potential, we first have to realize what is being transformed in us and the collective consciousness we inherited. Without that understanding, we remain blind to how we perpetuate the patterns of our mind that block us from rising to the greater potential of our heart. To put that another way, we have to see the truth of what has been operating in the world we created in fear before we can harness the full scale of our Divine power to create a world in love. Inherited aspects of our evolution are fascinating and richly nuanced from the Divine vantage point, and that perspective can help us truly honor, rather than ignore, the burden humanity has carried in our collective grief and guilt. We are releasing that burden now at an ever-accelerating rate, which is why our journey feels in many ways lighter as we progress, even amidst the confusion. Every single one of us heals and transforms our past in the present moment when we honor our truths.

To realize the truth of our past in the context of our awakening, several years ago I was shown how we have unknowingly perpetuated the cycle of pain in our world through our belief that we are separate from Divine Love. That belief inherently creates a desperate yearning for union with Divine Love that we can never sate from separation consciousness. I was assured that breaking this cycle is "the work of the Universe," but before the full scale of that work, and our part in it, can be understood, we have to realize that who we think we are is very different than the true Source of our existence. If we are indeed in a separation consciousness — aware of life through the lens of belief that we are separate from the Source of our life — then what exactly is this Source? What exactly is this Love with which we so deeply yearn to unite? I enter into the answer one day when I find myself where "I" began, and there was total darkness . . .

The emptiness of this darkness is an exquisite void unlike anything known on Earth. It is the purity of nothingness and the pure potential of everything.

I am here, simply aware. I am Awareness itself. And in this moment, I am aware of only two things: nothingness, and my singular nature. My nature is solely *cherishing*.

I gaze into this exquisite darkness weightless and rapt. I am not here inside some thing that is aware and cherishing. Cherishing Awareness is The Only Thing Itself. It is God. As both witness and that which is witnessed, perceiver and that which is perceived, I am simultaneously All and One.

I become aware of movement emanating from this darkness creating an aspect of God that looks like a massive colorless cloud of vibration. I can feel the energy of the vibrations and realize I am a point of awareness within this movement. I understand that this movement is how God can experience itself through "my" energy, and

"I" can experience existence through God's infinite potential.

With crystal clarity I am aware of the instant that I, *with and of God,* become aware of myself as pure joyful energy and want to experience *being* what I Am. As I feel myself engorged with the movement of God, a supremely powerful thought wells up within me: *I AM GOODNESS, AND I WANT TO BE ALL THAT I AM!* Like a rocket, these words propel me with tremendous force into the beginning of my evolution. The very moment I experience the proverb, "In the beginning was the Word and the Word was with God," I become God experiencing existence and existence experiencing God.

As a singular point of Cherishing Awareness, my longing to experience my own goodness is God's longing to experience its own goodness, or God-ness. The impulse of God — that which moves everything into existence — is the desire to be aware of and cherish all there is to be aware of and cherish. God seeks only to know Itself. It seeks only to BE all that It Is, not simply through *what* it is aware of, but all the *ways* it can be aware and all the *angles* from which awareness can occur. From omnipresence and omniscience to individuated aspects and every combination of patterns and perspectives of existence in-between, the potential for *being* is infinite and eternal. God can zoom in to be Awareness as of a single point of life, zoom out to be Awareness as multiple portions of life, or not zoom at all and simply be Awareness as all of life at once.

This game
of our life
is one-on-one,
between you
and the god
in your chest.

Grow that relationship
to the degree you desire.
How deeply
do you want
to embrace yourself?

TWO

PINK BLOUSE

While the idea of transcending separation consciousness to experience the unitive God state — *knowing* God in expression through and as us — sounds nice, how can we in our human form really be both perceiver and that which is perceived when we can clearly see reality as a separate thing outside of ourselves? I experience how this happens one night while getting ready for bed . . .

I am wearing a pink blouse I had tailor-made in India. I take it off and lay it over the back of a chair, then turn and walk a few steps across the room to pick up a t-shirt laying on the bed. Something compels me to turn around, and in a flash the entire room is gone and I am immersed in and as Oneness. Everything is an infinite range of colors and patterns moving in every direction, multidimensionally. And I am part of all of it. I am both witness and that which is witnessed.

From multiple perspectives simultaneously, I begin to watch myself taking in the patterns of color and movement through my left eye. It is an unfathomable scale of data I am simultaneously perceiving and being. I watch this stream of data travel with astounding speed through me, like following a flash of lightening as it streaks throughout my entire body and energetic field. I can follow all the patterns with perfect clarity as they engage with all the patterns that make up "my" body and field. And I can *feel* every turn of data at once. Within this data there are countless things working together simultaneously: mathematics, quantum mechanics, layer upon layer of historical references, even subtle emotions.

As I watch and feel this engagement of perceiver/perceived energies and the unfathomable scale of things working together at lightning speed, I begin to see how the data moving through me is being interpreted and translated into my perception of form. Every swiftly turning bit of energy within me is causing something akin to a pixelation of what I see outside of me. I watch from both inside and outside of "myself" as the room begins to coalesce into the gradual manifestation of form, space and dimensions, eventually creating the perception of a "blouse" laying on a "chair" "over there."

But even beyond the perception of form, space and dimension, I can also see all that came together in history to create the things I am seeing. In a flash, I see fields of cotton growing, then I watch weathered hands picking, weaving, dying and sewing that cotton until it becomes a "blouse" that is now "mine." Beneath the earth's surface, I see myriad nutrients being absorbed into the roots of the tree that became the wood that was cut and shaped and pieced together for what is now, in this room, called "chair." I watch humanity collectively agree to how we do these kinds of things, what we call these kinds of things, and how it all operates in various cultures. I see all of us share layer upon layer of this information in spoken and unspoken ways, shaping each others' worlds as we go through life in this richly connected way. And I can feel from the Divine perspective that every single bit of this experience is deeply, profoundly, *fascinating.* A sense of wonder and adoration courses throughout all of it. Every component of this perception — shape, size, color, distance, historical references, the connections within all of it — is created by both the patterns of data I am perceiving and the patterns of data through which I am perceiving. I see and feel it all from the perspective of being both perceiver and that which is perceived.

Truth will reform,
so beautifully,
every piece
of the orchestra
of your Life.

Energy will open within you
and the cosmos will quiver
as you align with truth's reeds
within you.

God will rise in you
like a standing ovation
applauding you
back into coherence.

THREE

MECHANISM OF CREATION

If we are really God in expression and God is really Cherishing Awareness, then how did we evolve to live in total blindness to this truth? The answer to this is revealed one day when I am pondering the question of how I was able to be propelled so spectacularly into the origins of "my" evolution with the single original thought, *"I AM GOODNESS, AND I WANT TO BE ALL THAT I AM!"* I grow deeply tired in my pondering and lie down to nap . . .

As soon as I lie back on my pillow a gorgeous symmetrical pattern of rotating atom-like energies comes before me.

The energies are extremely bright, like the glare of sunlight on aluminum, and mirror-like reflective. As I watch these energies move together in various patterns similar to a kaleidoscope, one core unit moves forward so I can see it in exquisite detail. The center looks like a ring of flower petals rotating counter-clockwise. Surrounding these petals are several circular rows of identical square plates, the edge of each slightly propped up on the one beside it. The circular rows of plates are all rotating clockwise. The last plate on the outer circular row is an image of me, happily smiling and waving.

As I take in this design I can see that I create my perception of physical form through the reflective interactions of the inner petals and outer plates. It's like bright mirrors moving around each other creating the perception of light in motion. I can see that the energy in the center, the rotation of the reflective flower petal pattern, is the movement created by the thought impulse, which in my original experience was my/God's desire to *BE*. This impulse moves the flower pattern petals to reflect onto the mirrored energies rotating around it, the circular rows of plates. This process of movement, fueled by the original thought impulse, builds hologram-like reflections back and forth, back and forth until the reflection finally transmutes my/God's thought into the perception of a "thing" that is *being*.

Understanding all of this, I realize that the inside flower petal pattern was created by the *focus* of my original thought: I AM GOODNESS! And the circular plate pattern was created by the *intention* of that same thought: I WANT TO *BE* ALL THAT I AM! This was the simple formula I experienced for the mechanism of creation: true focus + true intention = creation.

As this mechanism of creation occurs to me, my understanding suddenly balloons out enormously and I see the entire evolution of how Mankind built the world we live in. We have expanded our reflective energies with every new experience: we think, create, learn and expand, think again, create again, learn again and expand again. Along the way we develop numerous senses and modes of awareness to help us perceive more and learn more from countless angles, and in doing so we also create "things" like dimension and density and speed, which in their lower vibrational states create a perception of linear time and finite space.

We begin to discern the array of our creations in what we think of as an intellectual sorting of "this" from "that" and "I" from "other." As we do so we begin interpreting our existence in terms of contrast. (If we are red and our whole environment is red, we can only experience red when we encounter the contrast of, say, yellow.) Our big leap comes when contrast leads to the *idea* of God contrasted with NOT God, which we happen onto to the moment we encountered the pattern of vibrational movement we now call fear.

We had begun this evolutionary journey with the concept of contrasting "this is good/me, that is different from good/me" and now add the concept of "this is good/me, that is NOT good/me." And we experience this NOT good/me — this thing we label "bad" — as threatening because we are aligned with the vibration of fear. In fact, we are *identifying as* the vibration of fear. As we dis-identify with good/me and identify as fear, we begin to believe the idea that we are separate from God, inherently creating a consciousness — a collective mindset — that believes that there is existence other than Divine Love. This "false" existence in separation is perpetually fueled by the mind that is fear-based and fear-perpetuated, since fear can only thrive in fear.

Our original evolution was an exploration of the experience of our *being* God/goodness by contrast: understanding what it is to *be* with that which feels like our own goodness and what it is to *be* with that which feels different from our own goodness. This kind of being was rooted in innocent and eager intentions. As I watch us evolve in that same innocence and eagerness when we begin to identify as fear and explore contrast through that lens, I see us make a critical turn away from remembering our Divine nature as joyful beings. Contrast through the lens of fear led us to *conflict*. Our thoughts began to focus on surviving in conflict instead of on the joyful experience of contrast. With our focus perpetually on fear and our intention perpetually on protecting ourselves from all the "bad" threats around us, the mechanism of creation allowed us to create an entirely fear-based good-versus-bad reality that believes it is separate from the very Source of our existence. And the foundations of that good-versus-bad reality can be seen throughout all the foundational systems of our world today.

I wasn't feeling well
so I went to the soul doctor.

She looked deeply into
my eyes
and said,
"Ahhh I see.

I see a brilliant soul in a world
that hasn't yet learned
how to whirl."

FOUR

BUDDHA'S ENLIGHTENMENT

The nature of our fear-based reality, in which we perceive ourselves as separate from Source, was reiterated in a wonderfully succinct way in my first encounter with Buddha. He helped deepen profound understandings with just one simple metaphor . . .

I am in a meditation when an image of Mata Amma, the Hindu "hugging saint" comes into my awareness. I see her sweet smile, and let the image float away. Shortly an image of His Holiness the 14th Dalai Lama arises. I look at it only briefly, but that is enough. Immediately I feel a swift pull into the Dalai Lama's mind. As soon as I am firmly there, I feel another swift pull through him, out of him, and into the 13th Dalai Lama's mind. Then the 12th Dalai Lama, then the 11th Dalai Lama. Each time it feels like a "plop!" into and out of each mind. I continue on like this all the way through the line of Dalai Lamas, and when I reach the 1st, I feel a powerful leap out of his mind and into the mind of Buddha. I am here at the first moment he experiences what is traditionally thought of as enlightenment under the pipal tree.

I see all that Buddha sees in the expanse of All That Is. I become all the possibilities of existence and nothingness at once. I look at All That Is and I am All That Is. I watch the interplay between all energies, noticing the flows and the snags and the entanglements. I see how the consciousness of emotions courses and at times alters directions and/or stagnates. I embody all of this. It feels like bobbing in an ocean of everything without touching anything.

It is all and only absolute love and equanimity in the exploration of experiences that are at times falsely warped in perception by the snags and entanglements. In particular, in this flowing body of energies I see what appears like a boulder made of fear and I watch how people, which appear like individuated segments of energies, get caught on the boulder and can't get loose. Soon more and more people are caught there, and it is as though an entire world is created in what feels like a stationary place within the great endless ocean of flowing energies. To those stuck on this boulder of fear, it does not feel like they are part of all that is flowing. From their vantage point, the flow is not happening with or through them; everything is happening *to* them. So they remain stuck in fear, constantly striving to protect themselves from letting anything happen to them that would risk their survival. They have no idea that the only thing that has snagged them is their belief that fear is separate from All That Is.

I stay here with Buddha a while, fascinated, absorbed, soaking it all in. We are not interpreting or assigning words to any part of the experience, we are just observing and understanding. The moment I have the thought that I understand everything, Buddha himself pops up in spirit form in front of me and looks at me with deeply content eyes. He has no form, but it is clearly him. He is expansive, as though taking up much of the cosmos. He smiles with a playful, piercing joy that makes me immediately cry in

34

ecstatic happiness. Without using words he says, "See? It's fun!"

Your light and shadows
are an ecosystem
intricately connected
into one another
sharing nutrients
like love notes
between roots.

Tend to both —
this is how we grow.

FIVE

PERPETUATION OF FEAR

To realize just how deeply fear has shaped the societies, cultures and religions we have all inherited as part of our human experience, it was Jesus who one day took me inside the collective consciousness of different countries so I could experience just a small sampling of how deeply layered iterations of fear continue to govern the masses still today.

The event happened after three successive nights in which my dreams were filled with fear. I could not remember the details of the dreams when I woke up, but I vividly remembered each time feeling like fears of all kinds were processing through me as though my body was a sieve. During my meditations fear crept into my mind through vague hints of random insecurities and worries, as if testing me to see if I would take the bait. I had a powerful desire to sleep during the day when I could not focus on meditation and when I finally gave in I had more fear dreams. Shortly after I woke up on the third morning, I encountered Jesus and was told to go with him . . .

Jesus sweeps me up in his arms and we travel low above Earth, first to Israel. Here I am shown in meticulous detail the roots of the oldest, deepest fears in the hearts of the Jewish population and in the long-flowing mindstreams of government. The fear I see goes far, far beneath the current-day façade of righteous political posturing and rigid theological or academic postulations. In simplest terms, I see that these old fears originated in sincerely well-intended concerns about breaking what was thought to be God's laws. I understand that the details of those laws are not relevant; the point of this lesson is to see that the fear that has driven this population for millennia was originally rooted in sincerely compassionate intention. I can actually feel that intention in the hearts of those who thousands of years ago first grasped this fear tightly and created the foundation for today's defensive, conflict-driven mindset. As I take this in, I feel enormous compassion emanating from Jesus and flowing through me.

Intertwined with this fear in the Jewish population, I also see in fine detail the nature of a relatively newer kind of fear the Palestinians hold, which in simplest terms is driven by desperate fear of abandonment by God, Earth and Man. I feel the origins of this fear like a massive pleading to be held and understood and accepted.

Jesus and I next go to China. Here, again in great detail, I see what drives the government to control the masses in the way they do. The foundations of the original motives are both compassionate and fear-based. I see there is an ancient, deeply engrained fear that the masses will lose hope if things do not appear orderly and safe, and if the masses lose hope then there is fear of chaos and large-scale loss of control. This breeds a "justified" desire for power in leaders and reliance on order in the masses.

Jesus now takes me to Russia, where yet a different kind of fear drives the government. Here I see a much deeper self-serving fear seeded by rulers concerned for their own potential loss of power and privilege, which ironically resulted in a sense of personal freedom for the masses. The energy of the population feels rugged; proudly and hardily toughened from the dynamics that literally govern their life.

The knowledge of these fears and the way people are driven, controlled, and/or comforted by them is layered with countless nuances, like eddy currents and debris in long rivers of fears that affect the flow and direction of life in countless ways. In each country I experience the roots and impact of fear from the perspectives of both the governments and the people in totality as though I am living all minds and dynamics at once. In this way, just through this small sampling I see fear from the same universal perspective as Jesus sees it, compassionately understanding the innocence of original intentions. It is clear how these intentions gradually became entrenched mindsets of fear that have ruled all nations and determined in extraordinary measure how the world operates. And I understand this is the same way fear came to rule the minds of individuals everywhere: fear is the ultimate well-intended but blindly perpetuated hand-me-down from and to every human being.

"I used to have
a limited idea
about myself,"

said our Universe.

"I had become comfortable
identifying
with a small fragment
of myself—

I was attached to the belief
that I was just the solar system!"

43

SIX

MOUNT OF BEATITUDES

Although Jesus knew the innocence at the root of our perpetuation of fear-based suffering, even he could not shake our deeply engrained belief that Divine Love is something "other" than ourselves. I experienced this firsthand the day I was swept up in his arms, incorporated into his body, and two of us became as one standing on a hillside and looking outward . . .

I realize the location is the Mount of Beatitudes. To the right are people who had earlier gathered to listen to "my" talk. They are all leaving, and as I watch them walking away I am aware that none of these people have taken in my words to live as their own. Instead, they have revered me for having said the words. In doing so, they will rely on me for their wisdom rather than fully understanding and *embodying* the wisdom for themselves.

In this way they have set me, Christ, apart from them. I, Christ, was in the words I spoke, reflecting and illuminating the light within each of them. But because of their blind lack of belief in their own divinity, and reverence of me as something special and separate from them, they will remain unaware of Christ within themselves. I, Christ, cannot yet be *realized* in their hearts without their will to unite and heal the painful blindness of separation consciousness.

Cry the same full-skied tears
the clouds cry
that refresh the world
and nurture the roots of all things
that will one day blossom.

SEVEN

CRUCIFIXION AND BIBLE

Given that the Bible has played such a significant part in both laying out moral rules and trying to guide humans into deeper relationship with God, it is not surprising that the most profound experiences of how the collective belief in separation has perpetuated the cycle of mass suffering came to me through encounters with Jesus and Moses. These were not metaphysical events meant to cast blame or damnation, but rather to illuminate an uncomfortable truth: no matter our innocence, individually and collectively we must understand the consequences of our beliefs and choices. The first experience revealing this truth began as I stepped over a threshold that separated gleaming white light in front of me from a dark cave through which I had just walked. I looked down, hesitated, and with confusion saw that my feet were nailed to a board . . .

My gaze slowly travels upward and I become aware now that I am in Jesus at his moment of physical death. My feet are nailed to a long piece of thick wood. With my arms outstretched, my hands are nailed to a shorter piece of wood. My head is heavy and bobs in surrender to the weight. This cross upon which my body hangs is being dragged sideways along a dirt path leading into a courtyard. The path and courtyard are crowded with loud, highly emotional people.

In this body/mind/spirit as Jesus I know everything that has happened in the evolution of Mankind over untold millennia in history, and I see in great detail all that led to this moment. My death is not the result of a betrayal by a disciple or the ploys of a few people in power who feel threatened by my presence. It is instead caused by the momentum of a mindset that took ages to cultivate, perpetuate and deeply entrench. In the absence of widespread connection to the flow of God's love, it is a mindset of fear and conflict that has thrived in the moralizing, domineering leaders ruling politics and religion — and in the subservient masses that believed they were at their mercy.

I am filled with immense sadness that so many people will suffer and feel sorrowful because of my death, and my deepest concern and compassion is for those whose actions bring about the events of the day. I look out at the emotional crowd and say to myself, "These people do not need to feel sorrowful. They just do not know."

I take my last breath now and feel my spirit powerfully pulled up through my chest as though it is being sucked out. I break free from the constraints of my physical form and hover horizontally in spirit form over the shell of my body. No one knows I am still here.

Now, in fine, intimate detail I know the emotions present in the heart of every person in the crowd as though they are my own. I know who is filled with shock, who is filled with anger, terror, guilt, rage, grief, sadness, and so on. The vibrations of their grief and guilt are magnificently strong. In every heart, regardless of any other emotions of the moment, there is sorrow. I see this sorrow like a thread stretching from long before this day up through the hearts of all these people and far into the future, all the way into the hearts of current-day humans. The source of this sorrow is the belief that we are separate from God's love. Today will deepen and perpetuate this sorrow.

I say, "I need to ease these people's sorrows. I never did." And then I say, "This was to have been the point of reconciliation."

In a flurry of activity, I now see what happens in the future. I see quick and vast exploitations of my death. I watch bishops and cardinals and kings scrambling to carve out dominions in my name century after century. I watch countless genuinely well-intentioned people swallowed up in the very same mindset that caused my death, dutifully using my death as instructed by others to further perpetuate separation, fear and conflict with the wedges of guilt, judgment and sin. I see death and more death throughout the centuries in passionate defense of misconstrued understandings of my teachings.

I understand in this moment why there could be no reconciliation. It was not that there was no goodness within the heart of Christianity; of course there was. But it was the way that the goodness was used that perpetuated suffering. Entrenched in the mindset of conflict and fear, Mankind did not want a good Christ that healed. Mankind wanted a good Christ that conquered.

The day after the crucifixion experience, the lesson on the impact of misconstrued biblical teachings continued with Moses . . .

I find myself in a long hallway filled with numerous doors on either side. As I walk along taking in the variety of doors, I become aware of a door all the way at the end with white light gleaming all around it. This is the door I have been looking for. I run as fast as I can down the hall and as I reach for the handle a being of brilliantly luminous light opens the door, laughing. I know this being instantly and flush with ecstatic bliss and surprise, I love him so much. Behind him is a reception of several dozen supremely joyful, loving angels (light beings of varying indistinct shapes), and I know and love all of them.

All the angels are laughing at me teasingly because it has taken me so long to find them. It is like I am late to my own party. "I'm sorry!" I say, laughing with them. "I didn't know how to get here!" They say they have been waiting for me so we could share important information. "We couldn't get started without you!"

After a lengthy period of walking through the crowd receiving warm greetings, we all move into a shimmering white room and sit in a U-shape with me at the base of the U. I am wearing a blue plaid flannel shirt as though to distinguish that I am the one who is to do the earthly work. Shortly a majestic God-like being of bright white-gold light arrives and sits right in front of me. I later learn this is Moses, although as a being of light he has the intimation of form rather than a solid physical being. Moses puts his light-hands upon my shoulders and gently leans his light-head into mine. He waits a moment, then without speaking he slowly gives me these words telepathically:

"This world (meaning the physical world) was not created as we think it was. We can see conflict throughout this world – throughout. This world was created through the conflicts of the people. You can see this."

With speed that feels at once instantaneous and timeless, I once again watch the creation, evolution and expansion of our fear-based reality through the perpetuation of conflict. I both see and feel it as the fundamental way of life, perceived by all of humanity as normal and expected, as if that is how life is supposed to be.

"We did not begin with conflicts as are seen in the Bible," Moses continues. "Conflicts laid out in the Bible helped create and facilitate conflicts of our world. That is not how we started. We started with absolute love and peace. This is the point to which we must return."

There is a long pause to allow me to take all this in. There are countless layers of information coming into my awareness, as though I can see the impact and nuance of every single intention and action in the world. I say, "It's all so simple," and am about to continue with, "and we have made it so hard," when he begins speaking again with unfathomable love and compassion:

"All this time people have believed in the mandates of their religions. Nations have warred. Brother has killed brother. This was based on false truths. What people turned to in order to justify their anger they didn't know was wrong. They just did not know." There is another brief pause before he ends our meeting with, "True truth rather than false truth. Bring these words and the angels home with you."

Shed the skins
of every old god
in your mind~

The unlocked cage
is the open heart.
Your truth is its key.

EIGHT

JUDGE JUDY FILTER

After understanding the perpetuation of suffering in our fear-driven separation consciousness from the perspective of Divine entities in otherworldly realms, I began to experience this wisdom for myself here in this earthly realm. I could clearly see the myriad ways in which we humans just accept as a fundamental truth that this "I" we think of as "me" is separate from everything else. I began to realize this "false truth" in a blessedly lighthearted way one day during a walk in a park . . .

As I am watching the people around me, I suddenly enter into the consciousness of all of them and become aware that their minds are analyzing, labeling, sorting, organizing, and judging absolutely everything — the nature, the people around them, and themselves. Their thoughts are relentless: Is it good? Is it safe? Is it pretty? Is it better? Is it right? What will others think? Am I enough? Am I too much? What if . . . ? How does . . . ? When did . . . ? Why can't . . . ? She should do this. He shouldn't have done that. So MANY, MANY thoughts!

As I am inside all these minds that are incessantly relating to world and self through *aboutness*, I realize that the way our mind filters information actually holds us like a magnet in the belief that that which is perceiving is a separate thing from that which is perceived. Our chronic orientation is towards, or in relationship to, "other" in our separation consciousness, not by active choice but by oblivious default. We are conditioned into this belief in separation and then can't even fathom that it is not true. I giggle as I refer to this filter as "Judge Judy" in my head because it is only concerned with the facts *about* this ongoing case of life.

I am reminded in this moment that the "I" that I have always thought of as Mary is not true. My "I" identity is a product of my own Judge Judy filter holding me in the belief that I am a separate entity experiencing a reality in which everything is "other" happening around or to me. Being held firmly in adherence to this belief has prevented me from consciously realizing that everything is, in fact, happening *through, with, and as* what I now see clearly is just an idea of "me."

The light of God
is the only revolutionary

It's what we look away from
in each other's eyes

it's the light
that's too bright
to see
even within our own selves.

NINE

LIGHT OF GOD

A simple way to understand the difference in the way the mind perceives identity and life differently from how it all appears from the Divine vantage point was shown to me one day as I was contemplating what it means to be the light of God. I questioned whether this has ever been an actual light visible on Earth or if it is simply a radiant goodness that can be sensed through expressions and gestures. I was warm in my bed and about to fall asleep when before me came the answer to my question . . .

With my eyes closed two screens appear side by side directly in front of me. On one screen is "being God's light" from the experience of my mind. On the other screen is "being God's light" from the experience of my heart.

On the mind screen the scene is drab and extremely elementary. It is like a strange artificial re-creation of a masterpiece depicting everyday life, with simple scenery and stick figure people moving about in predictable, mechanical motion. It is empty of reality, but it is as though the mind is trying earnestly to reproduce its own concept of reality.

Next to this, on the heart screen there is ethereal wonder. Colors are otherworldly and vibrant, with a vibrating clear luminescence bathing every single aspect of the scene. Motions of both people and nature are fluid and somehow melodic. Feelings are felt like a breeze and drenched in compassion and understanding. All things in the scene are varying forms of vibration. In fact, the entire scene itself is vibrating, as though the finest movements of the space in which everything exists are visibly alive. In this scene I can see precisely how everything is intertwined. Everything affects everything, and in every impact there are magnificent vibrations of love.

As I watch these two side-by-side screens, I can see that the heart knows that to be God's light is to let go of all conceptual constraints and BE the full energy, or vibration, of what I Am. And that energy/vibration is all forms of light itself. I can also see that my mind cannot understand what that means – because the very function of my mind is to try to understand, and therefore it can never actually BE or re-produce what it is trying to understand. The mind therefore only – and always – produces a false reality. To be God's light is to BE only – and always – of the heart.

I fell into the void,
went through the dark night
of the soul-ar system
and came out to realize:

~what I've worked so hard to keep out
was always, already, eternally in

~we are all the wildly,
wonderfully diverse, Universe
ever-expanding into wider truth

it's time we get on
with celebrating that.

TEN

RECONCILIATION

At various points in the evolution of our awakening we begin to feel like we are "leveling up," though we usually can't say how or what that even means. I discovered I was apparently ready to start embodying the bigger picture of what is at hand in humanity's awakening one day when I recalled the line from the crucifixion experience when I was in the body of Jesus and said, "This was to have been the point of reconciliation." Even though I was recalling this line many years after the crucifixion experience, the moment I brought the memory to mind I was once again swept up in the arms of Jesus, incorporated into his body, and the two of us were integrated into the higher Christ consciousness . . .

I become part of a massive collective consciousness spanning all dimensions. I/We take up much of the cosmos and are descending slowly over and into Earth.

As I look out over parts of Earth, I speak as Jesus within this consciousness and say in reference to the time of "my" death, "We could have ended things then . . . the peace and goodness of the earth could have been. But Man made a choice." I talk at length now about Man choosing himself over God. "This battle, Man's battle, has always been about Man's will over God's gifts. None of what we see in this world today that is apart from peace ever had to be. Ever. As long as we continue to choose Man's will over God's gifts, it will always feel bad."

I shape two O's in the air by touching my thumbs to my curled fingers on each hand. I bring my hands together to form one large O and say, "Visually, the point of reconciliation was supposed to have gone like this, where we are separate and then come together as one."

I pull my hands apart and form the two O's again. I hesitate, then push them together solidly and say, "But what happened was we came together and went like this," then bounce the circles off and away from each other.

I raise the circle of my left hand. "This is Mankind," I say firmly. Then I raise the circle of my right hand. "And this is love and peace and joy and wisdom and caring and kindness."

"There are pieces that can overlap, but the overwhelming majority exists here," I continue, raising the Mankind circle again. "And this is a hard, conflict-ridden world."

I raise the right-hand circle once more. "And *this* is where we need to be."

I wait for a moment, then speak as the union of Jesus and Mary. "In this human existence I have been living in the overlapping portion in the middle of the two O's, and now, I need to be in God's O. I am to reach in and pull people through from Man's O to God's O. That is what I'm supposed to do."

Later I speak again as Jesus about the story of his life that most people think of as truth. I say, "My existence was not complicated. But I was not able to reveal that uncomplicatedness in the way that it needed to be revealed so that people could understand it. So people set me *apart from*, rather than made me *a part of.* And I meant to be a part of."

I recall now at the crucifixion seeing the thread of sorrow in the hearts of everyone that continued through to the hearts of everyone today – the sorrow of separation from God. I say, "The reason for the continuation of sorrow is because I, Christ, wasn't realized in their hearts. I wasn't a part of them to be able to continue. People see me as this distinct separation, and I'm not."

I speak now about "my" return, which is at hand, and say that this time it will be different. "This time I am not a prophet. I'm bigger. 'Presence' isn't quite right. Bigger. People didn't tell the true story about my life. Nobody here has that true story. So in that regard it's not really the Second Coming . . . it's the Coming."

68

Give me true intimacy
with God

No more of these formalities.
I want to holler my love at Her
from my kitchen
when I'm elbow deep
in dirty dishes

ELEVEN

AWARENESS RISING

As my understandings of the course of our past were about to give way to experiences of where we are now and what's ahead, Archangel Michael came to me one day to acknowledge this time of transition. He appeared to my left as glorious golden light. He was enormous in stature; even without distinct form he appeared strong beyond compare and exuded deep wisdom and kindness . . .

Referring to numerous losses I experienced over the years in my awakening process, Michael tells me that these losses were important. He says, "While it is hard, you do not "need" the things you think you have lost. You have other work to do. It is good work, is fulfilling work, but it is going to take time. That is where Love will be."

He tells me that he knows I have been ready for this work, but everyone else around me wasn't ready. "They're wimpy," he jokes. There is such immense love for me in his laugh it makes my whole body flush with warmth and comfort.

Michael says, "You have earned your robes," but I can see he means something other than robes, more like an apparel of light. As I am pondering this apparel of light I see "AWARENESS" arch over me, emanating from a large heavenly spotlight that is shining down upon me from behind.

"You are going to know things on a lot of levels," Michael says. "LOTS of different levels. Now it is going to get big." As he tells me this I feel myself backing into the heavenly spotlight behind me. It is as though I am backing away from Michael, but not in a bad way. He has work to do where he is needed and I have work to do where I am needed, which I understand now is where AWARENESS is rising.

There is a fine and devastating
untangling
of comfortable falsity
your soul must go through
to become anew.

TWELVE

WORK OF THE UNIVERSE

To take the critical step over the threshold from past to present in our awakening, it is not only our relationship to fear we have to fully understand, but our relationship to love. Throughout the ages, everyone from poets and saints to rock stars and life coaches have made "love is all we need" a household cliché. Some have gone so far as to say that, in fact, love is all there is. But if either of these platitudes are true, then why hasn't love ever been enough to make our suffering go away?

From a mystical perspective, the answer to this question goes to the root cause of the perpetual cycle of pain and confusion that has defined humanity's past. I began to embody this realization in a profound way through what was shown to me as "the work of the Universe." Early one morning I entered a dazzling celestial room and sat down in a chair . . .

A large sphere of diffuse gold light appears and floats before me. Without the light saying a word, I can feel it is simultaneously hysterically funny and intensely loving, as though it is tickling me and hugging me at the same time. I am delighted to the point of tears, and every speck of the light is thrilled by my delight.

Even though we appear to be separate, the light and I are, in fact, united. I am part of this light; it is the source of me, and we are both expressions of Source Itself.

The light has come in response to my request for help. For three months I have been feeling blocked, unable to move forward in any way with my work. It is like a writer's block where words just won't come, but what is not coming for me is any sense about what I am to do with my mystical abilities. I have repeatedly tried to feel my way around the block, to no avail.

It occurred to me one day that perhaps the block itself is my work. So, I began to meditate on it, feel into it on my morning hikes, contemplate its presence relentlessly. Today, in a deeply meditative state, this light has shown up to help.

When the giddiness of our mutual delight settles down enough to get to work, I ask the light, "Can you help me with this sense of feeling blocked?"

The light drifts forward and extends a portion of itself into my stomach. "It's here," it says. "Unquestionably."

I feel pain in my stomach and can see within me there is a block that looks like a bowling ball: heavy, dense, round. Instantly I understand with absolute certainty that this is a fundamental block in humanity, not just in me.

Quickly everything in my consciousness expands massively and I become aware of all that is within and around the block, including countless layers of nuances in the very concept of "block" itself. The enormity of all that is present at once is overwhelming and I cannot process or filter or interpret such scale. My mind hurries to try to narrate what is happening, but words are wildly inadequate to capture the depth of meaning of all that is here.

Unable to process the scale of the block using words, an image opens up before me: a gloriously vast cosmos in which, in galaxy after galaxy, love flows effortlessly in all directions . . . except in one spot. Suspended deep in this cosmos is a single round block through which no love is entering or exiting. The block is minuscule relative to its surroundings, but its importance is palpable. The entire cosmos is aware of this block, but nothing here can penetrate its boundaries because this single block in all the cosmos — the same block I carry within me — belongs solely to humanity.

"Whooaaa," I whisper in amazement.

I want to ask the light to help me understand what is happening, but the moment I turn my attention to the light, I lose awareness of the block. And when I return my attention to the block, I lose awareness of the light. I am unable to focus on the light and the block at the same time, and right now the block is seeking to be known. I smile to the light and say, "Thank you for getting me here," and it fades away.

I return my attention to the block and ask, "What is your nature?" Forcefully, the word SEPARATION rushes up within me. As I am taking this in, more follows: "OH, BUT I AM MORE THAN THAT. I AM ALSO THE CRY FOR UNION."

With that, an accelerated overview of humanity's evolution begins, starting with the creation of separation consciousness — our belief that we are separate from Source. I see the first moment we perceived a specific reflection of ourselves that made us turn away from, rather than cherish, what we perceived. That reflection was fear. In that critical moment of Self rejection, we turned our awareness away from our own Divine nature as pure love and recoiled in fear — straight into a fear-based separation consciousness.

A great swell of sorrow fills me as I watch our evolution. I see humanity in its illusory world of fear, everyone blinded by their belief that they are all alone while constantly crying out in desperate longing for union with God . . . without knowing that all the while they are already of God. It's like watching fish swim around sorrowfully yearning to know water. I can see clearly that the fundamental block for humanity is our belief that we are separate from the Source of our existence, and our relentless cry for union with the Source of our existence. We are expressions of Divine Love believing we are separate from Divine Love and deeply yearning to *feel* loved.

When the overview of our evolution stops, everything goes quiet. I wait to see if something else is going to happen but nothing does. Finally I ask, "Okay, so how can we get rid of this block?"

A powerful force appears and radiates from within and around the block, both protecting and strengthening it. My question gave the block enormous power. I realize now that the *idea of rejection* is the source of the block. The moment this critical understanding occurs everything goes quiet again but the realization reverberates through me like an echo traveling on and on and on.

I wait for the reverberations to stop, then expect something else to happen but nothing does. Finally I say, "Okay, I don't want to reject the block. I just want to understand it." With this, I begin to be pulled into the block. As I enter, my entire being expands like a balloon being inflated; I lose my "self" and become the block itself. As this happens, I become consumed with intense anger that is distinctly dark and ancient. I can discern countless other emotions in the anger, all of them aggressively teeming with resentment and defensiveness. I realize now that I am becoming everything humans label "bad" — fear, judgment, war, violence, self-loathing, rape, poverty, rage, jealousy, and so on. The scale of what I am embodying is unfathomable. I am literally experiencing the being of all that we think is bad in all of humanity.

Simultaneous to this embodiment, millions of words and concepts are flying at me from within the cosmos, bombarding me with far more information than I can take in. All the bad things are telling me the stories of their evolution at once. And in every single story — every single "bad" thing in humanity — I can see it is all just pain. Every single thing we label "bad" is simply a different iteration of pain. And in every single bad thing I can feel *profound* sadness. Because long ago we decided that pain is to be rejected.

With this realization it becomes clear that, since rejection is the very thing that gives this fundamental block in humanity strength and protection, as long as we reject what we label "bad" we are stuck in a self-perpetuating cycle of pain. We reject the pain born in our belief in separation consciousness, and thereby create more pain of separation consciousness.

Because this entire block is in perceived separation from Divine Love, it has no way to feel loved or comforted by Love, so it has to care for itself. It is the very energy of aloneness and loneliness in having to take care of oneself, as well as the resentment for having to do so.

All the stories slow down enough now to become like a wave and I see the original rising up of all that is created from the fear that makes us believe we are separate from Divine Love — judgment, inequality, blame, hatred, oppression, anger, and on and on . . . the list is endless. I see it all through the lens of separation and also see how all of these things originated in, and only exist in, perceived separation from Divine Love. And I realize that this is why I couldn't perceive the light and the block at the same time: because you cannot perceive both from the vantage point of separation consciousness.

I feel enormous resentment swirling in the block because none of this is understood and there is nothing taking care of all of this "bad" content. I struggle to assign words to all that's happening, and the very notion that I can't articulate what is here is part of the problem. With bitter anger I say, "Oh yea, everyone likes talking about all that nicey-nicey, lovey-lovey stuff. But no one wants to talk about *this*. No, *I* have to talk about this!" It is clear that this block is not attended to because no one wants to own its contents, and that is the source of much of the sadness and anger I feel. Humanity considers all of these iterations of pain unwanted "negative" and "bad" things, and in embodying all of this in my human identity I can feel a remarkably heightened sense of self-loathing, defensiveness and blame.

After a moment I look out at the block suspended in the cosmos full of love and say, "I want to dissolve this block with everything that's around it, which is all just love. So . . . why can't I do that?"

My stomach begins to ache powerfully. Defiance emanates from the bowling ball-like block within me and within the block suspended in the cosmos as well, but I can also feel something else that I can't quite identify. Numerous words swirl around until finally one rushes up insistently and hangs before my eyes: LONGING. Suddenly I feel every single thing in this block crying out *desperately* for union with love. It's as though everything is pleading, pleading, pleading for me to end this pain of separation.

In response, everything that I equate with love within me comes rushing forward to heal this block. Kindness, compassion, concern, empathy, it all moves urgently to the fore. And none of it can touch the block. I can feel my emotions physically pulling towards the block earnestly wanting to heal it. But nothing I consider aspects of love within me can get anywhere near it.

I now watch the entire cosmos cradle the block in Divine Love. Love swirls in all directions around it. I feel consumed with cosmic-sized compassion and eagerness to heal the block. Still, nothing can penetrate its boundaries.

I begin to get very upset. "Why not?!" I say. "WHY NOT?! This block is always, always, always, surrounded by nothing but love. Why can't love heal the pain of separation from love? Isn't that what we're crying out for?!" I pause, then say, "That's the ultimate question. That's the question I need to answer."

As I remain in the moment, staring out at the cosmos frustrated and confounded, suddenly the light of Source returns and asks, "Why can't you answer that question, Mary?"

Startled, I cannot speak. The light repeats, "*Why* can't you answer that question, Mary?"

The light is not concerned with the answer to the question of why love can't heal the pain of separation from love. It wants me to understand why I can't answer that question. And I have no idea.

As I am pondering this question, deeply confused, suddenly all of the atoms and molecules of the cosmos — every speck of the cosmos — begins to fill in with light. Divine light rises up everywhere like curtains of individuated vibrations and fills in every space. And all of this Divine Presence is magnificently serious.

From within this Divine Presence I hear, "This is the work of the Universe."

Before me now, the Divine Presence begins to project my body as though it is on a movie screen. I watch as they take my body through a series of simple movements: lying flat on my back, my right knee pulls up and circles clockwise three times, then counter-clockwise three times, and then my left leg does the same. The movement repeats again, to make sure I understand.

I am being shown that this is my path to dissolving the block. After the body movements, they show me that the dissolution process will be an absorption of the block into all the Divine energies that surround it. They use the analogy of a soap bubble: when the boundary of the soap bubble is pierced, then *POOF* the essence of the emptiness the soap bubble contained is absorbed into the Divine energies around it. Within me it feels like piercing the boundary of the bubble with a needle, and then the *idea* of it disappears on a breeze. The Divine Presence tells me that the absorption process is their work, but the piercing process is my work. While this all begins for me with the body movements, they tell me that the actual piercing will take place over several days.

I take all of this in, then say, "Okay. I understand. I have homework to do."

With this acknowledgement I feel a tremendous weight echo throughout the cosmos. It is the feel of a necessity, a determination, a firm decision that THIS. IS. IT. "There is no other work," I say.

The cosmos of Divine Presence responds, "There is this work, and all other work falls away."

I had my first taste of that sweet, sweet
love tonight for the Essence
that made all the innumerable tidbits
of majesty
sprouting from every wondrous pocket
of the sacred world

I had my first taste of Divine love tonight
and let's just say
I want more of that.

THIRTEEN

PIERCING THE SOAP BUBBLE

The homework portion of the fundamental block in humanity's experience — the soap bubble that requires piercing — was the first time I embodied the full breadth of what is underway now in humanity's spiritual awakening. The body movements shown to me by the Divine Presence were not the actual piercing itself but simply the key that unlocked the door to the realms where I could understand what my true homework was . . .

As soon as I begin the body movements, I feel something akin to an electric current coursing through me and extending out a few inches around me. As I move, the current rolls up my body and then back down. With each movement the current gets stronger and wider, gradually expanding exponentially far beyond the space I'm in physically. Shortly the current reaches into multiple dimensions including and beyond Earth. When it grows to the size of the entire universe, the current begins to bring in ancient information. And just as happened when I initially united with the block, that information is once again all the "bad" things that are born in separation consciousness — fear, judgment, rage, poverty, and so on. This time, however, I'm watching humans create these energies. I see us literally perceive, interpret, and define these things and then relate to them as "negative" energies as we build our reality. I watch us build each and every "bad" pattern of energy and *only* relate to it as something opposite to what we consider "good."

Watching this, I see how we use the scaffolding of a dualistic conquering mentality as our fundamental operational paradigm. I watch us use everything we label "good" — that which feels safe and not threatening to fear — to dominate, conquer, and reject everything we label "bad." In fact, I even watch us create the seductive allure of a conflict arc, adding dramatic tension to the dynamic interplay of energies by using the good to build up the threat of the bad so that the good can swoop in and be the hero that conquers the bad. We begin to highlight the good in contrast to the bad *specifically to highlight the conquering of the bad by the good,* over and over again. I watch us build our entire reality from the ground up using this paradigm.

As I am watching us perpetuate this good-conquers-bad pattern of creation to build all the foundations of our separation consciousness reality, suddenly everything fast-forwards to current day. Now I can clearly see that this is the dynamic, this is the very paradigm, that has paced the rhythms of our poetry. I watch it sweep ballet dancers dramatically across a stage. I see in the magnificent (and *required*) conflict arcs of our books and movies and stories. I hear it in the lyrics to our favorite songs. I see it eloquently threaded through religious doctrine. I see it used as the building blocks of our economics, our education, our governance, our sports, our cultural and societal systems — do more, be better, achieve greatly, be worthy, be successful, be obedient . . . all to overcome the possibility of being something *bad.*

Watching all the systems of our world built on this good-conquers-bad dynamic, I see why history is framed in terms of heroes. It's why the world loves the stories of overcoming, winning, conquering. This dynamic is so cleverly engrained as normal in our consciousness that we even see cartoons and Disney movies as wholesome and healthy even though they fundamentally depend on the tension of a conflict arc in which something good conquers or overcomes something bad. We see performance pressure as necessary in education lest we be defeated by ignorance, and necessary in sports and business lest we be bested by competitors. Conflict is a revered part of our heroic stories whether it is dressed up in military fatigues, grades, profits, or fairy princess gowns.

This model of reality has conditioned us to stay on high alert, constantly striving and judging and achieving our way into safety and wellbeing. We must be good and diligent, lest we are bad or susceptible to the threat of bad.

As I see all of this happening, I remember the answer when I asked the fundamental block in humanity what its nature is: SEPARATION, AND THE CRY FOR UNION. In this moment, I realize that every single one of the things that we label negative — every single "bad" thing — is a loud cry for union with love. These things have always been our most painful cries for love.

As all of this information swirls within me, I experience the understanding that, because the human concept of love is equated with that which we label "good," we mistakenly believe that we are being loving when we use our good to try to make our bad go away. What we have never understood is that this is not healing. This is rejection born of the conquering mentality. And rejection is the very thing that gives the fundamental block in humanity — separation from *Divine* Love — its power. We have been using our good-only version of love like a weapon to conquer the bad, when all this does is reject our cries for union with love and keeps the cycle of pain going.

This is not just rejection of the world around us. It is a rejection of God. It is our own Self rejection. Because we are, in truth, all Oneness. When we think we are bringing in love to make a bad pain go away, what we're actually employing is a model of one part of us trying to make another part of us go away. And it is clear from our history that we can't. No bad we see in our world today just started. We just keep recycling and expanding it through the cycle of rejecting our pain and thereby creating more pain. Pain has never once wanted to be rejected. It has only ever wanted to be loved.

The answer to the question of why love has never been able to make our suffering go away is that the human idea of love, born in fear and wielded as a divisive rather than uniting ideal, is not love. *It is the very thing perpetuating the cycle of suffering.*

Our good-only version of love, which was my own version for most of my life, is why in the block/soap bubble experience I couldn't answer the question of why my love or all the love in the cosmos couldn't make the pain of separation from love go away. My idea of love was to make the block and all the bad things go away. And that is not love. While my earnest desire was well intentioned, it was still rejection. *Divine* Love is embracing, not rejecting. It is healing, not conquering.

This is not to imply that kindness, empathy, compassion, and all else we equate with human love is wrong; we are not now making these things the new bad. The key to understanding what love really is — *Divine Love* — is in the sincerity of our intention. Are we really seeking to love *divinely*?

As all of the pieces of this experience are coming together in my awareness, I profoundly feel the sorrow and weight of our cries for Divine Love. I know very well what Divine Love is; I have lived it many times through the body of Jesus, the mind of Buddha, the light and evolution of God. This love is not an action. It is a state of being.

In Divine Love everything is unconditionally accepted as it is because it is *of God*. Everything is equal in value and potential, free to be whatever it is, as it is, without resistance or rejection or judgment. In Divine Love every single thing is *seen and understood* as a precious aspect or expression of Oneness. Everything is honored as part of the truth of All That We Are, and it is that sincere recognition that *heals* every kind of pain, every kind of "bad."

Realizing all of this in the deepest core of my being, I now understand what finally pierces the block/soap bubble. The body movement exercises were only meant to get me to this understanding. The actual piercing of the fundamental block within me and within humanity can only happen when I get my own state of being in alignment with God. I need to be in direct alignment with my own Divine nature. I must become the Divine Love I am — that WE are — crying out for.

With incredible clarity of purpose, I say firmly, "Anything that comes into or arises in my field I will accept

91

unconditionally! I will impose no conditions on *anything* to exist in my field. Anything that arises in my field will be accepted as an equal in value and potential and possibility to exist! Everything that arises in my field is free to express what it is, as it is, I will not oppress or resist! Everything that arises in my field will be brought into a state of unity and oneness with every other part of my being! I will accept in this present moment whatever arises in my field!"

The moment I hit the mark; the moment I am in direct alignment with my own Divine nature and present as a Divine vibrational field, all that we label "bad" in separation consciousness starts coming around again. But this time they come one at a time. And the first thing up is fear.

When fear hits my Divine field there is a massive energetic explosion. Every kind of fear imaginable blasts throughout my awareness. I can feel the purity of every tiny nuance of every kind of fear imaginable. And every bit of it is "mine." It is every speck of fear I have ever had in this lifetime, in my entire existence, and in all the ways I have ever entangled or interwoven fear in the collective consciousness of humanity through my rejection or resistance of it. It is a spectacularly pure expression of all fear I have ever known and all fear humanity has known because of me. Ever.

Within every speck of this fear, I feel the devastating pain at its core. I feel all the pain I have held in my lifetime, my existence, and in the collective consciousness of humanity because of my relationship with fear. The scale is unfathomable. I am stunned beyond words. I think of myself as a nice person, and yet look at all this pain I have perpetuated! Compounding my shock is the fact that every speck of pain I can see is like a living entity looking right back at me knowing I have rejected it.

I begin to sob and sob and sob. I heave tears and repeat, "Oh my God, oh my God. I'm so sorry. I'm so, so sorry."

After processing my profound shock and remorse to the point of emotional exhaustion, finally all I can say is, "Please forgive me." It is a request to myself, to the fear, to the collective, and most of all to the pain. As soon as the words "please forgive me" leave my mouth, there is a *POOF* in my field and all the fear and pain vanish, absorbed instantly into healing union with Divine Love. I have pierced the soap bubble.

Immediately there is another explosion in my energetic field. This time it is judgment. Again, it is all the iterations of judgment in my lifetime, my existence, and in the collective consciousness of humanity that I put there through my relationship with judgment. Again, the unfathomable scale of pain. Again the sobbing. Again the "I'm so sorry." Again, the "Please forgive me." And again, *POOF*.

Then another explosion, this time of self-loathing. Again, the same exact process. Then rage. Then war, and so on.

The piercing process goes on in this manner day and night, day and night. Sure enough, just as I had been told by the Divine Presence, all of it takes several days. Some "bad" things take several hours to process, others take only a few minutes, and a few come back around for deeper healing. When I finally reach the end of all that I can heal at this time for myself and the collective, I walk out of my room at the nunnery where I am living in the Himalayas and see the world very differently.

Everywhere I go, I experience in people's energy fields and in their consciousness all the ways they are living with Self/God rejection. And I can feel every bit of their unanswered cries for union with Divine Love. Every field and consciousness seems to communicate with me, and it all appears like white flags waving in surrender. Emanating from everyone I see are the words, "I'm ready. I'm ready for a world in healing."

PART TWO

WHERE WE ARE NOW

PRAYER FLAGS

The work is finally moving
out of your parents' house
to God's house.

Pack up all the baggage,
the loads of dirty laundry
you collected there

and have dragged around
your entire life
gripping tightly to your past
like a doctrine
and finally take it all over
to unload at God's place.

The Beloved will unpack it all with you,
shake it all out,
and you'll both have a good laugh,
"Where did you get this strange number?!"

Then God will clean them off
and hang them to dry
on a line in the sun—
making them all prayer flags.

FOURTEEN

JUDGE JUDY RETIREMENT

As my metaphysical experiences progressed into understanding what *is* happening in humanity more than what *has been* happening, one night I had a fun dream that reiterated the transitional stage that is at hand . . .

I am at a crowded party in a castle. I walk alone from spacious room to spacious room watching smartly dressed people chat in small groups. Everyone appears to be having a lovely time; they lean in as others speak, smile, and listen attentively.

As I enter through yet another doorway, someone behind me taps me on my shoulder. I turn to see a woman I do not recognize but she seems to know me. She says, "Judge Judy wants to see you."

I follow the woman down a gold-walled corridor and into a magnificent room in which Judge Judy is holding court . . . but in a musical way. She sits behind an ornately-sculpted judge's bench, high above the crowd. To her left is a large band in which all the musicians are wearing tuxedos. When Judge Judy sees me enter the room she motions to the band to start up, then she nods towards me and says to the crowd, "She's going to take over for me now. Watch."

I have no idea what she is talking about, but as the music begins I walk over and stand to the side of her bench. The band is playing the old George Gershwin classic "'S

Wonderful," and Judge Judy begins singing, "'S wonderful, 's marvelous . . . "

She looks at me adoringly as she sings. After the first couple of lines she motions for me to join her. Much to my surprise, we sing fabulously together. But halfway through the song she gradually stops and it is just me singing — and I am really belting it out. I do not know the words, they just flow from me powerfully on their own.

Judge Judy beams proudly as she watches me. When I finish the song she turns to the crowd and sighs with a satisfying nod. She turns back to me, smiles knowingly, and steps down from her chair, retiring forever.

The sacred wears a good costume.
She loves to dress up
as the ordinary.

Sometimes, like a queen
in peasant clothes
She cloaks herself in the mundane
to get a break
from all that fawning.

FIFTEEN

I AM

When I began to deeply understand that we are in a gradual process of aligning evermore with the truth of our Divine nature and integrating that True Self into our conscious state of being, my metaphysical events kept reiterating just what that True Self is. This was important, because it was easy for my mind to keep falling back into small, separate ways of self identification. It was particularly helpful that these reiterating metaphysical events put me directly in the "I Am" scenarios to *experience* the Message of Truth that I Am . . .

I AM CHRIST CONSCIOUSNESS

I am part body, part spirit. My body is the front part of a massive cosmic spirit. I have a body because it is the part people can see, the thing that people can understand. It is what people can concretize and make sense of. But I am connected to this massive spirit-presence, which is the consciousness of Christ. The consciousness of Christ and I are one and the same.

Behind me is a sky crammed full of white lights shaped like origami-styled doves. Jesus is at the core of this Christ consciousness I/we occupy, so I inquire of him: "Who are these beings behind me?" Jesus tells me these are the souls I am to lead to a peace and happiness they have never known. These are the souls I am to lead to Christ.

I AM THE WAY, TRUTH, LIGHT

I am standing on a road made entirely of pure truth. I stand upon this road as a body of light made of the same pure truth. All the people of the world are behind me and I am about to lead them down this road.

In my physical body I feel pressure from a bolus of energy stuck in my chest. I focus on the area just below the block and imagine gently forcing the obstruction to move or dissolve. While doing this I become so nauseated I have to fetch a bowl and paper towel in case I throw up. I try now to be still and just let the energy do what it will. Shortly I feel movement in my chest, and with astonishing clarity I become both the image and the wisdom of the image of the road of pure truth, my own light of pure truth and the world behind me that I am about to lead onto this road.

I Am the Way, the Truth, and the Light.

I AM PORTAL

I am cradled in God's embrace. I feel It all around, holding me. I feel Its intention to let me know there is safety in the truth of my spirit and All That Is.

As God holds me I become rich, burning gold. I am here on Earth but also in an expansive blackness of Divine Love, sitting on a large ornate chair that has a tall, wide back like a throne. I place my hands on the arms of the chair and look around.

I am taking in the blackness that is enveloping me when I become aware of light below me. I peer down through a floor that looks hazy as though it is some kind of thin veil and see numerous beings of light busily passing to and fro. The area appears to be a transit station of some sort. I am aware that these Divine spirits are able to be here in this earthly realm and do their work because of the access I provide through the space I occupy right now, and because of my own presence in said space. I am a portal through which they can integrate into this reality.

While watching this activity, something catches my eye to my left. I look over and see a formless God smirking at me in an ornery, teasing kind of way. I laugh out loud with shock. It is showing me there is fun here as well as seriousness. Without words I hear It say in a playful gotcha! sort of tone, "You weren't expecting that, now were you?" The love and adoration for me is so unfathomably pure I burst into tears.

I AM THE LIFE OF CHRIST

I am in a silent, vast, exquisitely black void. There is a subtle movement in the distance that appears like a soft vibrational ripple. Slowly the ripple becomes more pronounced and closer, until finally I feel it enter me. As that happens, a vibration of words rises up:

These are the words that come from the place of perfect love and wisdom. These are the words to BE, from the heart. These are the words to be taken in and lived.
~Jesus

105

I Am the Way of Love, the Truth of Love, the luminous Light of Love.

Where the rhythm of awareness beats in the heart, I Am Christ.

Where trust prevails and fear is no more, I Am Christ.

I Am pure compassion, kindness, and wisdom.

I Am absolute peace and love.

I Am all possibility.

I Am all.

I Am.

***

I Am within: For each, I am found in the shell of no other. Where there is unity with the Love within, I Am.

I Am the soothingly rich depth of the quiet mind and the vast knowing flowing through the heart. When the mind and heart reconcile to the truth of oneness, I Am.

No scripture or sermon is necessary to live according to Love. Every heart knows the way. The very current pulsing through every heart is Love, and in Love there is no other admonition than to BE Love. I Am this Love.

***

I Am Equality: I Am the Truth that all are equal, for all are One. Equality does not mean conformity. All aspects of life are by their very nature unique aspects of Love that are equally precious and beloved. All give life to Love and Love gives life to All.

I speak as Love beneath the sounds of fear and judgment. I Am the Truth that judgment is in direct opposition to unconditional Love. Where unconditional Love is opposed, there is suffering. Where unconditional Love flourishes, I Am.

Where the roots of conflict are pulled up and seeds of unity are planted, I Am.

***

I Am Forgiveness: I Am the recognition that there is nothing to forgive.

I Am above and below no other and therefore make no judgment of another's rightness or wrongness. I Am the understanding that there is nothing to be right or wrong about. There simply is, without meaning. Meaning is assigned in the mind of Man alone. I Am the true compassionate understanding behind the false façade of meaning.

***

I Am Intention: I Am the intention of Love. I Am the intention behind every thought to BE the goodness of Love. I Am the intention of compassion and kindness behind every word and deed. I Am the intention to BE Love.

***

I Am Reverence: I Am that which reveres no one but Love, and even that in gratitude alone. I Am the BE-ing of God's life, which is Love, and all around and within me are equally Love.

***

I Am Commerce and Community: I Am the currency of compassion and caring. I Am the exchange of Love for Love. I Am the Divine tender of joy, sustenance, experience and support. I Am the thrill of nurturance, the passion of empathy, the undying devotion to Love in All. I Am that which releases the shackles of slavery and exploitation. I Am that which heals blindness to one's own worth, unleashes one's own potential and in eternal freedom allows one to live according to one's own joyful expression of Love.

***

I Am Passion: I Am the passionate Love within Me. I Am the passionate Love for Me. I Am the passionate heralding of My spirit and soul equal to that of all, which is equal to Love. I Am the passionate celebration and embrace of all life equally, for all life is wondrous expression of Love.

***

I Am Gratitude: Above all, I Am gratitude beyond compare for the miracle of all life, for life is Love living itself.

***

I Am Now: All the endless interpretations of my past are moot. Right now is all that matters. There is nothing in my evolution that is more important than this moment. I Am Here. I Am Now. What the world thinks of Me – any version of Me – based on the past is irrelevant. The past separates Me from the present and is therefore of no use. I am only to be known now; there is no other way.

***

Final words: All will know me. At first some will be scared for they do not understand what is happening. Then they will be surprised when they realize what is at hand. Then they will know a peace and happiness they have never known. They will know me, Christ.

There is great love coming . . . like a great tidal wave . . . like the force of a thousand winds. It is unstoppable.

You should welcome it when it comes.

Finally, the gay pride parade
of nebula
began doing their all
to defy
the law and order
of drabness
insisting this universe
include a broader and more nuanced
spectrum
of brightness.

SIXTEEN

WE ARE: SUE

Among the countless realizations I have had along this awakening journey, one in particular took me a very long time to understand because I had no frame of reference for it: we are not evolving out of separation consciousness on our own. We are doing this — *must* inherently do this — together. Our awakening has to happen in union with others because what we are evolving into is evermore realization of our Oneness.

What this means practically is that we begin to share and/or expand our consciousness with others, not just in this earthly dimension but across multiple dimensions. This is, in fact, what happens in all of my metaphysical experiences, and it is what happens in any spiritually transformative or near-death experience when someone encounters information in other realms or other beings. In these experiences we expand our awareness and share consciousness beyond the confines of our separation reality. We are reaching the stage in awakening where we can experience God-as-us zooming in and out to be aware in multiple ways.

These experiences are occurring more and more throughout the world. Our abilities to connect to Divine realms and wisdom are increasing not only in the frequency of occurrences but in the diversity of occurrences. On our path to Divine union we are beginning to encounter physical and non-physical beings alike that serve multidimensional purposes, and we do the same for them. We are becoming like open doors — literal portals — with and for each other in this earthly realm and across any number of dimensions, even when we or the other parties are unaware of what is happening.

The first person with whom this happened for me was my friend Sue, several years before I started to come into my metaphysical abilities in any significant way. It began one afternoon when my then-partner Kerry and I were at a cafeteria in a mall in Little Rock, Arkansas . . .

We are making our way down the buffet line facing the trays of food choices when I am suddenly overwhelmed with a knowing that Kerry is about to meet Sue, who had recently become my therapist. I turn and look around, but Sue is nowhere to be seen. I say to Kerry, "You're about to meet Sue!"

Kerry turns and looks around, too. "Where is she?"

"I don't know," I say. "But it's about to happen."

Kerry looks at me curiously, smiles with a shrug, then we continue moving down the buffet line.

Several minutes later, Kerry and I are in the dining room of the cafeteria eating when I see Sue and her husband walk in and head to the restrooms in the far corner. I point her out to Kerry, and sure enough, on their way out Sue and her husband stop by our table to say hello. They had been shopping in the mall and stopped by before heading home just to use the restroom.

A few weeks later, I have an appointment at Sue's office, which is located in the back of her hilltop house. I park my car at the bottom of the hill where a path leads up the woods to the back of the house. As I turn off the car, in an instant I am in the body of Sue. I am still me, but I am in the body of Sue and experiencing exactly what Sue is doing and feeling. She is working in a garden, hot and sweaty, and she is blissfully happy. My own body begins to sweat and fill with bliss. I can feel Sue's hands moving around in the dirt, and I can feel the grime of dirt and sweat on her skin.

I sit in the car wildly shocked, feeling sweaty and grimy and blissed out, trying to make sense of what is happening. After a few minutes I manage to open the door and get out of the car, and as I walk up the path the body-consciousness sharing experience gradually fades away.

Once at the back door I ring the doorbell but there is no answer. I ring again, no answer. As I turn to go around to the front of the house, Sue rounds the corner, wearing gardening gloves. She is red-cheeked with sweat, and positively beaming with joy. "Oh! I'm sorry!" she exclaims. She looks up at the sun and continues, "I was in the garden playing in this beautiful sunshine and lost all track of time!"

Six years later, it was Sue whom I called to ask for help because strange mystical things had started happening to me. A week after that call, Sue was standing right beside me when the gates to my metaphysical abilities flung wide open.

I want for you
the merriment
of wide open meadows
longing for your dance

I want for you
connection
with the spring breeze
that plays with your hair
and delights in you.

SEVENTEEN

WE ARE: LISA

The second earthly person with whom consciousness sharing played a key role in my understandings was my friend Lisa. Our fascinating union started when I began writing my first book, *Unwitting Mystic*. It had taken me twelve years to be ready to talk openly about how I went from being a staunchly agnostic healthcare executive living in Washington, DC to being a mystic living in a Buddhist nunnery in the Himalayas. It was painfully difficult for me to talk about the uncontrollable mystical experiences I kept having, in part because the details of these otherworldly events are almost impossible to capture adequately in words, and in part because I was embarrassed and afraid to confess to having such experiences. Dealing with both of these issues became much easier when I finally started writing *Unwitting Mystic* and a delightful cheerleader-type spirit showed up to help. In the book I wrote of this helper:

"Within just a few hours of working on the new manuscript a formless, transparent spirit appeared before me. It felt like an adoring grandmother, a wise guardian, and an ornery childhood friend all rolled up into one. The spirit cupped my cheeks in its "hands" and telepathically said very excitedly, "Yes, yes!" It was powerfully encouraging and upbeat energy, and it thrilled me so deeply I had to squish my face up to absorb all the joy. The spirit appeared in the exact same way again and again, at

least thirty times over the next few months, always at a time when I was working on something I felt needed to be handled particularly delicately. It was like a cheerleader keeping me company and a monitor keeping me on track."

At the time this started happening I was away from the nunnery visiting my sister in Texas. When I decided it was time to return to India to finish the book, the moment I made that decision the spirit appeared to me again, cupping my cheeks and excitedly saying, "Yes, yes!" as it always did. But when I made the flight reservations to New Delhi something different happened . . .

The moment I finalize my reservation and the confirmation pops up on my computer screen, the spirit appears, this time laughing joyfully. To my deep delight, the spirit tousles my hair and playfully kisses the top of my head. Beaming with love, it says, "See you there!"

In India, as I continue to write the manuscript from my room at the nunnery, the cheerleading spirit continues to show up at key points in the process, always cupping my cheeks with a joyful "yes, yes!" No one at the nunnery knows I am writing a book, and only a few nuns know about my metaphysical experiences, so this cheerleading spirit is very much my little secret.

One morning, one of the other nunnery residents, Jampa, comes to my door and asks me to accompany her and another resident, Lisa, to the hospital. Lisa had fallen on the rock path leading to the nunnery and busted her chin open. I had lived in India long enough to know how to navigate the frenzied chaos of rural emergency rooms, so Jampa asks me to go with them to get Lisa stitched up.

I have seen Lisa around Thosamling for several weeks, but before this day we had never met. She is staying at the nunnery while taking onsite Tibetan language classes because she is an English tutor to exiled Tibetans near the Dalai Lama's temple in the village of McCleodganj; she figures she can be a better tutor if she speaks their native language. Most residents at the nunnery know about the smart American student who is the size of a ten-year-old child but has the smoky eyes and luxurious locks of a Hollywood actress. She keeps to herself most of time, so I only see her occasionally in the dining hall and at residents' meetings.

Lisa, Jampa and I spend several hours in a taxi and then the emergency room getting Lisa fixed up, and we return to the nunnery after lunch. I tell Lisa I have salve in my room that will be good to put over her freshly-dressed wound, and I bring it to her room a short while later. Her door is ajar, and from across the room Lisa tells me to come in. As I step over the threshold I am jolted by a recognition so startling I stop in my tracks. The feeling is instantly transporting in the way only something deeply familiar can be, like the smell of a grandmother's face cream or a favorite childhood melody. I *know* Lisa. She is the cheerleading spirit! How had I not recognized her before? We had just spent at least three hours together and I had felt no inkling of her spirit aspect whatsoever. But now in her personal space it is undeniable. My mind is reeling with questions, the most pressing being: does *she* know she is the cheerleading spirit?! Should I say something?! Lisa appears entirely unfazed, so I pull myself together and decide to say nothing until I can think things through.

I see Lisa around the nunnery for several days afterwards without any engagement other than an occasional hello or head nod. One evening she shows up at my door with one of the resident nuns, Venerable Pelyang, who is having trouble with her Mac computer. Lisa has been trying unsuccessfully to help Pelyang, and since I have a Mac computer they came to see if I can help.

The two come in and sit on the edge of my twin bed, and I pull up a plastic chair to sit beside Pelyang. The three of us have been gathered in my room like this for less than two minutes trying to fix the computer problem when I say something that unexpectedly delights Lisa. To my shock, she jumps up, tousles my hair, and playfully kisses the top of my head — exactly as the cheerleading spirit had done when I booked my flight back to India. The inside of my head swirls so fast I feel faint.

Lisa gives no indication in this moment or in the days following that she has any idea we have an otherworldly connection. I am nearing completion of the manuscript and Cheerleading Spirit Lisa is still showing up, while Human Lisa is still staying to herself. The secret of the two Lisas is weighing heavily on my heart; I very much want to let her in on what I know, but to do that I first have to tell her about my mystical abilities. Since we aren't really friends there is no easy way to strike up a conversation that can lead to that intimate of a reveal.

I write the final words to the manuscript for *Unwitting Mystic* on a Wednesday just before the 11:30AM lunch bell rings. After typing the last word and clicking "save," I close my computer with dramatic flair, feeling a sense of accomplishment coupled with disbelief. The book has taken five months to write and it feels right in every way. I really want to celebrate with Lisa since part of her has helped me every step of the way, but we still haven't connected and she doesn't even know I have been writing a book. So, when the lunch bell rings I head to the dining hall thinking about where I am going to take myself to dinner tonight.

On my way to the dining hall, Lisa is coming from class and we intersect on the path. We pass each other on this path almost daily, but this time, for the first time ever, she stops to talk to me. She is thinner than usual because she has been sick for a week.

"Hey," she says. "Maria (a Finnish student in her class) and I are going to dinner tonight at Himalayan Brothers in Sidhpur. Do you want to join us? I'm better and I feel like celebrating."

It hasn't been two minutes since I finished a manuscript that Lisa has no idea she helped me write. She has no idea I have been walking up the path feeling like celebrating and that I really want to have a celebratory dinner with her.

I smile and say, "Sure! I'm in."

Days later I spill the beans to Lisa. She never had any inkling of what was happening with the spirit aspect of herself, but the experience bonded us in a dear friendship that continues to this day. She continued to cheer me on after *Unwitting Mystic* was published and I began doing book tours in the U.S., and over the years I have helped support her on her spiritual journey. She eventually began having her own encounters with Divine realms, and today spiritually transformative experiences are a normal, ongoing part of her life.

You don't have to have
a spiritual path
but do run
the most sensitive
part of your soul
over the soft curves
of this world
with as much tenderness
as you can find in yourself
and let her edgeless ways
inspire you to discover more

EIGHTEEN

WE ARE: CORENE

The most significant and ongoing demonstrations of the diverse ways that consciousness sharing can happen have been revealed through my relationship with a woman named Corene in Brisbane, Australia.

Corene and I first met after she saw an online interview with me and reached out to offer support. In addition to her background in law, academia, psychotherapy and hypnotherapy, she has had a lifelong interest in spirituality and the esoteric. Perhaps this was why, during a meditation a few weeks after seeing my interview and subsequently reading *Unwitting Mystic*, she heard a voice tell her to reach out to me.

To give you an idea of the profundity of experiences that happen when Corene and I connect, the extensive metaphysical experience involving the soap bubble — my lesson on the fundamental block in humanity — happened the first time Corene and I met. Notably, that meeting happened online; she was on the coast of eastern Australia and I was in the Himalayas in India, and through the virtual medium of the internet she was able to help quiet my mind enough to explore the significant block I had been experiencing. To this day, despite the fact that several of the events mentioned in this text happened while I was in connection with Corene, we have never met in person.

There are no boundaries when it comes to ways to share consciousness.

A new level of consciousness sharing began when Corene and I connected two weeks after the COVID-19 pandemic got into full swing. We were in an online meditation together, just as we had been doing weekly for several months, when something within me instructed me to yield my focus . . .

As soon as I let my awareness recede, a large arena full of light beings appears. They say, "We are to be called Consensus. This is not to be confused with finding a lowest common denominator and considering that a consensus. On the contrary, we are the highest note possible in this moment." Consensus then begins to harmonize their energies, and a distinct vibrational "note" rises up throughout the arena. It feels like a powerful tuning fork being struck, and the translation of that vibrational note begins to be narrated through me.

Unbeknownst to me, this is the beginning of what will turn out to be a series of profound teachings addressing what is happening within humanity, what is still to come, and how to stay steady as the chaos of the awakening momentum continues. Importantly, these channeled teachings not only come through me, but also through Corene. She, however, receives the teachings in richly visual scenes rather than narrated words. We consistently receive the exact same wisdom, just perceived through different lenses. Select experiences with Consensus are included in several subsequent chapters of this book.

Corene and I have yet another level of consciousness sharing demonstrated for us eight months after our cochanneling experiences began. Her mother, Anne, was dying of pancreatic cancer and had lingered for weeks in a horrific near-dead state. Her seeming inability to die baffled doctors and was a daily source of deep pain for Corene and her five siblings. Anne's life expectancy was only three weeks at the time of her diagnosis, but in the eleventh week there was still breath in her tiny, unconscious body that came in shallow gasps every eight to ten seconds. With no allopathic options working, Corene asked me one evening if I thought Consensus might be able to help her mother transition. I told her I had no idea but we could make the invitation . . .

Corene is by her mother's bedside in the hospital when we connect via video chat. There is no one else present. Corene turns the phone around so I can see her mother, and I tell her who I am and what we are going to do together. "I'm going to invite in some Divine help for you, Anne," I say. "I'll tell you everything that's happening as we do this." I take several breaths, invite in Consensus, and then wait.

Shortly I feel Consensus come into the energetic field we all share in that moment. They hold the field very still, connecting with Anne with supreme tenderness. In less than a minute I feel my awareness pulled into Anne's throat. Although she appears unconscious and her eyes are rolled up in her head, I can feel she is present and trying urgently to say, "I'm sorry." I relay this to Corene, "You're mom wants to say she's sorry." Corene bursts into tears, strokes her mother's head and tells her that all is okay. Anne's body and breath instantly soften.

Now I see Jesus come forward from the arena of Consensus and walk around to the other side of Anne's bed. He places his hand gently on the back of her head and says, "I'll be her companion to take her home." He keeps his hand on her head for a moment, then walks back around and sits down on the bed between Corene and her mother. I say, "Jesus is going to take you home now, Anne." With that, I bid her and Corene goodbye so they can be alone. Less than five minutes later, Anne takes her last breath.

Two years after this shared consciousness experience between me, Anne, and Consensus, Corene is walking down a street in Brisbane, Australia and realizes that, at will, she can enter the consciousness of any stranger she sees. It begins when she unites with the consciousness of a young man entering a coffee shop and Corene instantly "knows" him and that he is anticipating what is going to happen inside the shop. After a moment she pulls her focus from him and enters into the consciousness of a woman entering a grocery store. Corene again "knows" this woman instantly; she is sad and her heart is burdened. Corene does this with five different people, each time with great ease, as though it was a practiced, everyday occurrence. At the same time, she can also see herself from a higher perspective watching her "small self" walking about learning that she can direct and expand her consciousness. She is having multiple layers and angles of awareness simultaneously, and is acutely aware in each occurrence that it is all a higher "Me" having these diverse experiences.

Corene's ability to enter into the consciousness of others remains to this day and is ever-increasing in frequency and ease.

I collected all
the sweet stars
into my chest
tonight—

darling, don't you know
we can be that vast?

Yes, the great magnitude
of our love
is what The Universe
is expanding into.

NINETEEN

WE ARE: WAKING OTHERS

A new avenue of sharing consciousness began to reveal itself after I woke up one morning into an instruction that I was to work with select individuals one-on-one in a way I had never done before. I saw myself immersed in a field of "open" consciousness with one individual at a time, nonstop over several days so that something akin to a shared passageway could develop and the other person could enter into their own Divine realizations and metaphysical abilities. The individuals were not identified in the moment, I was only to understand that it was time to offer "private individual retreats" and trust that the right people would come forward.

I began offering these retreats to people in my private community just two weeks later, spending five days in a remote location in nature with one person at a time. We started each day with no plan whatsoever except to go into a meditative state together multiple times a day and allow Divine guidance to come through. My role was simply to sit across from the other person and remain in a yielded state. I began each session with a silent, "Love will guide from here," and then spoke only what rose up as words to speak or images to convey in my perception. This allowed Divine guidance to come first through me and then through the other person if they were able to relax their mind enough.

135

Most participants experienced an incredible range of healings and realizations, not just for themselves but for the collective of humanity, and they were repeatedly able to connect to higher realms of consciousness. The variety and depth of these experiences are illustrated through three retreatants who graciously allowed me to share a bit of their stories. Entire tomes could be written about the stunning scope of wisdom revealed in each of their retreats, but these snippets can provide a glimpse of what happened.

The first story comes from Julie, who owns a dog-boarding business in Olympia, Washington . . .

I have been working one-on-one with Julie in a remote cabin for four days, during which time she has experienced dozens of profound realizations about herself, her family, and overall fundamental truths about life. By this time she has released an incredible amount of fear in her body and mind and she is able to connect with Divine realms on her own with ease. During an afternoon break on the fourth day I am inside the cabin and Julie is somewhere outside. While making tea, I become aware of a heavy emotion that feels like it is literally hanging in the air. It feels like deep grief and sorrow. Up to this point Julie has done an amazing job of processing all emotions as they came up, and the session we just ended was not particularly emotionally intense, so I have no idea why there is such overt heaviness present.

Thinking that perhaps something is happening with Julie, I go outside and find her in a hammock by the river in front of the cabin. I settle into a hammock next to hers and nonchalantly ask how she is feeling. "Sooo peaceful," she says. "I'm just watching the light on the water."

"Excellent," I reply. I relax in the hammock for a minute then ask if her mind is quiet.

"Totally quiet," she says. "*Amazingly* quiet."

"That's what we love to hear," I say lightly. I stay for a while longer then tell her I'll see her back in the cabin shortly.

As we are settling into our seats for the next session, the instant we close our eyes to enter into a meditative state I am guided to tell Julie to tune in to the first thing she can sense. I say, "Pay attention to what rises up in this moment, without thinking about it, and whatever it is speak it out loud please."

Julie takes a breath then says, "Okay, I see a field." She pauses, then continues, "And now there's a steam."

"Good," I say. "Just stay with the stream and see what happens."

After a moment Julie says, "There's a little girl in the stream. I can feel memories of this child; she is feeling the magic of this stream and has a sacred connection to it. She loves to play here."

Julie's expression changes from calm to concern. She says, "But there's something else here that feels really intense. It's a strong sense of pain and grief around the loss of innocence. It has to do with something deeply painful that has occurred at the hands of a man."

At this point I assume Julie is about to work through a childhood trauma of her own. But this is not correct. Much to the surprise of both of us, Julie is connecting with an enormous trauma in the collective consciousness that she is about to process on behalf of all.

Julie starts to cry. "The stream is filling up with many little girls who lost their innocence. And women, too. So many women." As the enormity of the grief unfolds, Julie begins to sob deeply. "There is deep collective grief here because of the loss of innocence of so many little girls and women. It feels like an endless well of grief." Julie's body is shaking as she processes the weight of such intense emotion. She begins to wail. "So much rape, torture, pain. So much confusion. Parts just feel frozen."

After a few minutes Julie's tears begin to slow and I see her body soften. She says, "Oh, there is Divine healing rising up now. It's coming through deep acknowledgement of the pain. It's all being seen through the lens of eternal wholeness." She takes a few breaths, then continues, "The pain from loss of innocence is being redeemed. I can feel all these same girls and women now in the Divine space with a sense of knowing their original wholeness. They are being reconnected to the aspect of themselves that has never been, and could never be, harmed."

After allowing plenty of time for Julie to let all this settle, I ask her if there is anyone left behind in the stream. This question arises because I myself am seeing men in the stream. Julie looks confused, then surprised. She says, "Oh. Yes. Oh my God!"

I ask, "Is it men?" As soon as I say these words, Julie again wells up with intense emotion.

"Yes!" she cries. "These men have such *immense* pain! I can feel their immense shame and self-hatred. They lost their innocence, too. They desperately long for the very same innocence I felt in the young girls. They have felt so completely cut off from all love and everything life-giving that they either wanted to consume or destroy the innocence. Our cultural conditioning of 'soldier training' men had them so disconnected. They have had to continually shove down their feelings while getting further and further disconnected from wholeness and love. They have such great pain in their sense of unworthiness, shame, and desperation for love and belonging."

Julie breaths out heavily several times, overwhelmed with compassion as she remains with the men. Shortly a figure appears. "There's a woman here now," Julie says. "It feels like what could be called Divine Mother. She's walking around the men and touching each one of them on their heart and then at the center of their forehead like she is anointing them." Julie raises two fingers and makes small strokes in the air as though placing marks on the mens' foreheads. "Divine Mother is invoking the remembrance of their original innocence. Their goodness and wholeness became so lost in the darkness, but these truths have always remained as a small flame in their heart that could never be extinguished."

The second story comes from Ashlee, a psychotherapist in Maine . . .

By the time Ashlee and I meet in a remote cabin it is mid-summer and she is in her sixth month of "long COVID" after testing positive for COVID-19 over the winter. She is young, independent, heavily tattooed, and previously had a kind of hardy badass energy about her, but now she has been plagued with chronic extreme fatigue and respiratory issues, and has been on oxygen for weeks.

Unlike Julie's retreat where each meditative session had its own focus, Ashlee's experiences unfold from the beginning in more of a building block manner to create a powerful fully-embodied presence of her True Self.

In one of our first sessions, Ashlee enters into a very deep meditative state and finds herself relaxing in the stands with Consensus in their arena. She knows Consensus well because she has been present for all of their teachings over the past two years. Here in the stands among these light beings, Ashlee sees herself as a beautiful, innocent maiden much like the Virgin Mary at a young age. Speaking from this vantage point she says, "I can see that all the language around "being strong" and "like a warrior" that has defined me in the past is actually egoic armor I have built up over the years to protect myself. There's an image of my True Self in this, and this 'I' is like the potential within a seed rather than the protective hard shell around the seed." At this point she says she sees rose petals floating across the sky on a gentle breeze. I ask what purpose these rose petals serve. "This is the image I can use to access my True Self anytime I need to."

We discover that Ashlee is able to enter into Divine realms and connect with deep wisdom remarkably fast when using a simple tool: writing on a notepad with her non-dominant hand while in a meditative state. I simply guide her to write something that requires her to finish a sentence, such as, "My higher self would like me to know . . . " and then she writes the answer until she begins speaking out loud in what becomes lengthy and profound orations of wisdom from Divine realms she has entered into.

These orations begin to relate extensively to the nature of truth, reality, and her True Self after she enters into the cosmic consciousness of a network of stars and discovers her soul's "origin" family referred to as The Mothers. "I am one of The Mothers," Ashlee says. "The other Mothers are associated with the heart, throat and crown chakras, and I am associated with the third eye. This is why I have the ability to access information about the nature of truth and reality."

The wisdom Ashlee brings forth in every session is so extensive, by the end of the first day I start audio recording her sessions because in each one so much unfolds it is all far too detailed to try to remember. Over the following days she effortlessly narrates more than eleven hours of stunning wisdom covering everything from Self-birth to the structure of vibrational communication within and across dimensions.

Ashlee does not use her oxygen at any point during the retreat. She regains her strength and vitality by the third day, and never has any respiratory or other issues related to COVID-19 again. Five months later, in the same week that Corene began entering into the consciousness of others without effort, Ashlee begins doing so as well. Realizing she has this ability, she now does energy work with others in a "True Self state" and is able to connect to others' higher selves, and assists them in making that connection for themselves. To her surprise, she discovered she can also help people connect to loved ones. In one instance, while with a friend who had experienced several significant losses, Ashlee felt a powerful energy surge come through her own body, enter her friend's body, and then her friend began communicating directly with three people she had lost. Ashlee says, "I seem to be able to hold some kind of field for people to begin accessing their own gifts. If they are too cut off from themselves, I can access that part for them and start to connect them to it."

In other words, she is a portal for others to access multidimensional states of consciousness.

The third story is from Cheri, a retired global utilities strategist in New York . . .

Just as happened with Ashlee, Cheri's experiences are immediately so profound and detailed I have to record every session to keep track of the unfathomable scale of things that are coming up. She, too, experiences the full scope of Self realization, from her origins within God to the part she plays in her soul group, and how these roots play out in her human expression. These extraordinary roots begin to reveal themselves in the very first session on day one within minutes of both of us dropping into a meditative state together with no guidance except to be still and simply allow.

"I'm at the edge of a gathering, hunkered down in a ball on the floor," Cheri begins. She waits, then continues, "I feel courage rising up now, and I'm standing at the edge." She waits again, then says, "Each time I get more courage the veil thins a little more . . . okay, I'm able to enter the gathering now, and the veil is gone. I feel like I belong. This is my soul group. There are five us here: Compassion, Strength, Joy, Love, and I am Connector. We are the nature of God's expression, and I am the part that *connects*. There is a ceremony going on, and we're all joined through the heart with energy that forms a pentagon shape given our positions. The energy is a golden red that glows and extends with long tails that we each tie into knots. Compassion is particularly strong, with an iridescent blue light running through her invitingly. Compassion is on my left, Strength is on my right. Joy and Love are the farthest away and they say they will return for more collaboration later in the retreat."

Things unfold so quickly, by the second session Cheri can tune into various vibrational tones, express them vocally, and then enter into the dimension that the tone is connected to in the multiverse. This allows her to *become* stunningly discrete details and narrate complex matters such as the nature of light, the relationship between frequency and perception, what happens inside the amplification of vibrational movement, and so on.

On the last day of Cheri's retreat, a channeling comes through me, intended to help Cheri see why things have unfolded in the way they have in our time together. I narrate: "Let us understand the scope of all that has happened in this retreat. The full scale of your Self-realization has spanned from your origins as Connector with the soul group that makes up the nature of God — Love, Joy, Strength, Compassion, and Connection. These are all parts that *emanate* from Source. They emanate all the way into the human expression of that Source, that Self, uniting everything in Divine Love. This retreat has been the point to which everything in your life has been leading: the recognition of Wholeness, and both the willingness and the way to *BE* all that you are."

Consensus then invites Cheri into the arena with them, where on the stage stands a single microphone. All parts of Cheri in her human life, many of which have shown up in the retreat deeply afraid to be seen, now take the stage. The first thing to step up to the microphone is Abandonment. It says, "Thank you, Cheri, for my freedom." The next thing up is Fearless, which simply comes forward so it can be seen "dressed to the nines." Worthiness steps up next wearing "an outfit of her own choosing" which includes a sage green dress and a single feather earring. It, too, is content just being seen. Eventually Cheri's family, friends and husband are invited into the arena to see all parts of Cheri standing proudly on the stage. This is her unabashed "coming out" to everyone as her True Self in human form.

You are the vibrations
of Divine Music
and you are
Her quivering reeds

disrobe your truth
and enter yourself
completely.

TWENTY

YOUR UNIQUENESS IS PRICELESS

On a weekly basis I channel Consensus in online gatherings with my private community, and before we enter a meditative state together I usually give a few remarks to talk about anything relative to the upcoming teaching or anything I have realized in the previous week. In one session during the COVID-19 pandemic, I was aware that we were at a stage where, because everyone had been cooped up for so long, people's minds were getting bored with a focus on stillness. To help the mind feel like it had something to do, I offered a list of suggestions that would engage the mind gently while also fostering continued energetic openings. One suggestion was to do creative new activities that involved the use of color, like painting or coloring. Both the newness of the creative endeavor and the vibrancy of colors would be stimulating for the mind, but not in a way that would add any burden or pressure to perform. It turns out that this was a welcome setup for what Consensus wanted to teach; they could use the topic of colors to help everyone understand the beauty of their unique contribution to what is underway for humanity . . .

"We are delighted to join this gathering this evening. We are most pleased that there was conversation leading into this about colors. That is fun. The idea of a colorful gathering is lively. It feels lively to each of us, to all of us.

147

Our sense of color is much more vast, unfathomably so, compared to the human understanding of colors. There is a rich continuum of every shade, not just the shades of a continuum of color, but each shade has a shape. It has a particular movement. It has a particular beautiful pattern. It has a particular relationship with all that is around it. In the human world we tend to think of color as a simple visual stimulus, when it is in fact so much more. This is the way of everything. Every sound. Every person. Every idea. Every belief. Every moment. You see, we are guiding you into the uniqueness of everything here. The glorious, wondrous, uniqueness of everything. Of all being.

"As you feel that recognition of the infinite uniqueness of all life, you can understand the precious nature of the transformation that is underway, that is heading towards everyone realizing this gift. All of humanity is awakening to that understanding. And as that awakening happens, we awaken into the celebration of that uniqueness. The wild embrace of that uniqueness. You can see why this time in humanity's evolution is so thrilling from the Divine perspective. It is exhilarating because it is such a gift to realize the scale of such beauty, of such extraordinary possibilities.

"Now, we will remind you that you have beautifully and willingly become anchors for the new. You can imagine a large stake being driven into the earth, driven all the way down deep into the earth; imagine the stability of that stake as a foundation. This is what you and this collective field are here for: foundations for all that is new, all that will be created. When we say 'will be created' we simply mean all that you will be coming into in the awareness of creation. When you imagine yourself and this field as a large stake driven deep into the earth in great stability as an anchor, and you yourself have the understanding, the appreciation, the knowing, of the profundity and beauty of uniqueness of all life, this is what you are anchoring.

"Remember, you are anchoring in union with Earth, which itself recognizes all of the uniqueness. Now, realize that anything that is built upon this anchor has this recognition as its foundation. This is the *starting* point. Do you see how extraordinary that understanding, that foundation, is in what it fosters and allows for the new? Do you understand the level of celebration, the level of appreciation, the level of awe, the level of eagerness to see more? To explore more, to allow more, to embrace more? This is you. This is what you are anchoring on behalf of all. Do you see why we have such adoration and cheering and gratitude for your willingness?

"We understand fully that in the human experience there are day-to-day issues that must be addressed, must be dealt with. But we will remind you that every day you wake up different than you were the day before. And in this awakening process now, from minute to minute to minute you are different than you were a minute before. You are different now than before you began this session.

"As each situation in life comes along, they are situations tethered to the past, tied to past situations, past relationships, past responsibilities, past tasks, past jobs, past beliefs, and your unique perception of them now is from what we might call a higher perspective. You are engaging with the old from the present; from the new present, if you will. You have a much greater capacity again and again and again to see things differently, to interpret things differently, to receive the information differently, and most importantly, to react differently. You have the ability as well as the willingness to take a breath, to check in to this field of knowing, to all of the uniqueness within this anchored field within, and respond from that place. You are able to embrace what is here from that place. You are able to allow something new to be created from this place.

"Now, that does not mean that a new reaction will always feel spectacular. Or that the world is suddenly all bliss. We will remind you that we are in a process of honoring everything. Every single energetic pattern and whatever is carried in that beautiful pattern — which is never a single thing by the way — will be honored. It will be felt. You can imagine standing in a doorway, things passing from one side of the door to the other. You are that doorway, but as it passes through it's embraced in your arms. You look at it, you see what it is, and you offer it into the new. You are both the portal through which things are processing and the new into which things are processing. You are the transformed as well as the transforming. And regardless of how much this may feel like a stumbling adventure, you are doing it perfectly. There is no doubt that to the human mind this feels like a mess. This is a gloriously beautiful mess and none of you have been here before. So you don't have the manual for how to clean it up. You are the cleaning up. You are that which says: I love this mess.

"When you have gone deeply inward, you can celebrate the newness that you feel within. This unique moment that you *are*. Celebrate in absolute wonder and giddiness the newness that is going on. You can be in a place of stillness and calm and anchoring, and things can still be difficult and a mess. And you can still be celebrating the transformation. In that way you miss nothing. You miss not a moment of love. Not a moment of cherishing. Not a moment of healing. Hear that. Hear that very clearly. Coming into this anchored place, the willingness to feel into all that's going on, the uniqueness of all that is happening with you, in you, as you, allows you to not miss a moment. It allows you to not miss a moment in this extraordinary time in humanity's evolution. And every moment that you are extraordinarily present, you accelerate the transformation for the collective.

"Remember that how you are in each moment is your contribution to the collective. You see how powerful you are? Throughout the cosmos you are being celebrated. You are being heralded again and again and again simply because you are here. You are here in your willingness. You are contributing to the collective in this way. And you are doing so perfectly."

Join me and let us be keys
to unlock every closed door
inside of us where latent
expressions of God have been waiting
for a tender enough space
to come forth
to sing life awake.

TWENTY-ONE

UNLOCKING PRISON DOORS

In every channeled teaching there is not just the sharing of wisdom but a transmission of energy that alchemically shifts consciousness. Given that Consensus is an extremely large collective of light beings, they must transmit gently so as not to overwhelm me and those in my private community with whom I and Consensus gather. They do this in an incredibly effective way by uniting with everyone in gradations of intensity to help all participants acclimate to their energies. We all enter into a meditative state together and Consensus teaches in energetic union with all participants while meeting each person where they are in their individual capacity and willingness. They work extensively through our bodies, moving energy vibrationally as they speak to give our energetic fields time and space to integrate. This allows all participants to understand through *visceral* awareness; we are brought into the embodied *experience* of the wisdom. A wonderful example of this is in their teaching on unlocking prison doors, which they delivered slowly to all of us in a deeply meditative state . . .

"The theme of this teaching is UNLOCKING. It is our pleasure to be here in this gathering that is rich in love and gratitude. We will speak tonight on the subject of unlocking. In the history of suffering within humanity there are countless patterns that have been created and bound tightly within the collective field, then passed down and practiced extensively in separation consciousness. These patterns that are bound, or tangled if you will, are what is experienced in this reality as pain. There is a way that humans feel imprisoned by the suffering without an ability to be released. This is what suffering feels like in the human experience. There's not just one kind or form of suffering, there's this suffering and that suffering and this other suffering, and then there is deeper suffering and deeper suffering. You can imagine a prison cell within a prison cell within a prison cell within a prison cell, and so on.

"In the awakening process, people have the frustration of feeling like they've already dealt with one particular kind of suffering and then it comes back around again. The prison cell is still there within another prison cell. In the awakening process, as one continues again and again to come into the body, come into the silence, into the stillness, into the calm, into the present moment, one is accessing again and again the key. Not just the key to the first prison door or the second prison door. But the key to the idea that there is a prison. So the key unlocks *that* door.

"Every pattern, every cell block if you will, has been imprinted in the energetic field. And every imprint – every single imprint – can be released as easily as opening a door.

"We speak slowly in this teaching so the body can have the experience that we speak of as we speak: the feeling of releasing the imprint of the pattern by the feeling of opening a door. That door opening is happening right here, right now, in this present moment. There doesn't need to be any specific identification of a pattern that we wish to release. We could be here for months listing out all of the various prison cells within us, within our energetic field. All that needs to happen is to use the same key, a single key, for every prison cell.

"We become that open door within us in this present moment. We become this with our awareness focused slowly, with deep intention, on the presence of this field in this moment: our body as it is, our presence as it is, this collective field as it is. We simply feel open. In this openness, no matter what is in the field, everything is equal. Everything simply is. Everything is free to be whatever it is, as it is. There's not an expectation or a need for anything to be different. There's both the allowance and the acceptance. There is only openness. There is only the state of unlocked.

"In the state of unlocked, the state of *being* unlocked, there is a recognition that we have complete control over our willingness to allow this state of being as our go-to presence. And our go-to response. This state of being is entirely effortless. This is the state of no doing and no fixing. We're simply allowing the openness itself to do all of the releasing, all of the unraveling of old patterns if you will. All of the doors are open. There's absolutely no need to retrace our steps, to go explore cell by cell by cell and talk about the whys and the hows and when and what with each and every single cell block. All the doors are open. You are the key. And the hand that holds that key is your willingness.

"We will remind you that this is an integration process. As energetic fields shift, the need for overt intentionality decreases over time as you become accustomed to simply walking in this state, *as* this state of being. We will also remind you that there is no need to be in any hurry; you and the collective learn from every step along the way. That does not mean that it's a painless experience. As these old pains come into our awareness, these old cell blocks of suffering, we will feel that pain. In a recent teaching with Corene there was the example of these painful patterns or experiences being like barbed wire in the flesh of the body where we hold these things. To pull that barbed wire out is sometimes painful.

"You are here specifically at this time in humanity's evolution, and in this gathering following the teachings of Mary and Consensus, for the healing not just of yourselves but each other and humanity. We are ready to unlock all of the prison doors at the origin point, the creation point of prison, cell, and door. Remember that we are all the key.

"We'll encourage you to feel into your body in this moment to be aware of all that you are allowing; to feel into the openness within you and within this field. You may feel the desire to lean into this collective field where we ourselves are harmonizing. We are in this moment assisting you in anchoring the memory of this into your own fields and into this collective field. We encourage you to make accessing this openness and this memory a repetition as often as you think about it. You can simply drop in. It doesn't have to be a ritual of any kind unless that's what feels good.

"This is entirely an energetic shifting. There's nothing uttered in this teaching for the mind. The mind is included in that which is embraced in this openness. It has no burden of having to do anything.

"Now, as this field is opened, it is not just the prisons of suffering that are released into the field of love. It is also creative potential. So we encourage you to stay open to the impulses that change, as small or as large as they may be. This concludes this transmission. We thank you for this love and for this gathering."

What kind of damn fool
puts off heaven?
Child, it lives in the center of your heart
that endless meadow of happiness
and praise.

The world needs you
to go there now
to do your part
in turning it
into a paradise.

TWENTY-TWO

EMBODYING THE TEACHERS

One of the most surprising points in this awakening journey came when Consensus guided members of my community to embody the Divine teachers. The night before this particular gathering, Consensus gave the following instructions to me: "Participants may use any teacher they choose: Jesus, angels, archangels, the whole of God itself, whatever they wish. They are to see themselves as that light, and then know relationship to Self from that vantage point. So, let us take Jane as an example. It will be Jane envisioning herself as, let's say, Jesus. What is the relationship that I have to myself now? An important part of this exercise is genuinely feeling themselves as that teacher, feeling the visceral sense of that light. That presence. That being. That state of mind. That state of love.

"What this exercise does is essentially call in that remembrance within the body. Then there will be a conversation with that presence. In addition to serving the purpose of shifting people into a higher sense of Self, it also serves to calm the body, mind, spirit, and psyche. As everything calms and begins to bring in this remembrance, participants have the ability to see the pointlessness of all the old stories of small, separate identity. Those stories are seen in a different light through this relationship.

"Now, we've spoken about trust and faith previously, and this lesson in part directs us to the questions: Do I really have trust that this is possible? Do I really have faith in all of this? You can see how multi-layered this lesson is and its benefits.

"However, the bigger benefit is that as each person calls us, the teachers, into them through this teaching, they also call us into the collective. So once participants reach the stage of softening and clarity, where they have a sense of wonder and curiosity, we will add this simple step: They are to embrace all of that clarity, wonder, and awe, take a nice deep breath in, and then radiate all of that out into the collective.

"The work of the anchoring begins now in a new way. What's important for the participants is simply the focus on using the teacher. We want to reiterate here that what is being addressed is a core level of fundamental change in life. This is a fundamental change in the way that individuals choose to live their life. They can make a conscious choice to live free from the suffering inherent in the pain of separation consciousness, free from the judgment and the fear and all of these other things. They can make a conscious choice to live in their freedom. As anchors, this is an important thing for them to realize. They have this choice. They are the presence of that awareness. There is the choice, not at an intellectual small self level but at an embodied True Self level. You can talk to any number of spiritual people in this world and they will say yes, sure, of course, we know we have the choice. But this is putting that choice to test, not at the surface but at the foundation.

"We want to be sure that you understand the idea of sinking into our presence here. If anyone is not able to feel the energetic presence, then you may simply imagine being in the presence of, let's say, all the archangels that you've ever heard of, all of the gurus and teachers from throughout history. Imagine that you're gathered with them. Let yourself be in that space and feel the truth that's present there. Feel the purity of that truth. Feel the purity of the love. Feel the purity of compassion. Feel the purity of existence. Now, we want you to hear us very clearly: In the presence of all of these teachers, why are they present? Why do you know about them at all? Because they've only ever been here to serve humanity. They've only ever been here to help, to guide, to comfort, to shepherd. Now realize: you are among them to help, to guide, to comfort, to shepherd. Do you see what we mean about sinking into *being* Divine presence?"

As Consensus is giving me these instructions, I understand exactly why they are having all participants do this exercise. When they said, "Why do we even know about the teachers? Why have they ever been here? It was only because they're here to help humanity," they were helping us understand what is living *through us*. The presence of these teachers IS us. We are the way, the avenue in for them. This is what I have been doing since the first moment I began waking up: bringing teachers into this reality through me. And since, in Oneness, every teacher is simply a representation of higher aspects of ourselves, this is how we begin uniting with evermore of our own Divine wholeness. Their instructions to me were an insistence that the gathering with my community was going to be *their* gathering. This was *their* moment. This was our own higher aspects announcing: we're HERE, NOW.

In a previous gathering, Consensus had said in a serious tone that while they are with us in love and joy, they are not here to play. "This isn't a game," they said. "This is a real-life thing that's happening. This is real work that's underway with real impact, and there are real consequences to our decisions, our choices, our willingness." They have been telling us all along that we are at the pinnacle of the time of transformation. They have been building things with us slowly, telling us that the reason for anchoring in calm, still, steadiness was to become anchors for the new. All along I have been thinking how nice it is that we get to do this for our own benefit while we also get to help humanity. But now I realize that it has never been just for us or for humanity. It's for *them*. Consensus and all Divine teachers, all higher aspects of Me/Us have been laying the foundations for themselves to come here through our human vessels. The anchors we've created are to anchor them into this realm through us — not in a mentalized way but in an *embodied* way . . .

The day after I received the instructions from Consensus I gather with my community and take everyone into meditation, guiding everyone to "Feel yourselves now as the invitation for Consensus. For guides. For all teachers. For all those who are eager to be in this reality with, and as, and among us. Welcome their presence. Feel yourselves completely open and allowing."

Quickly Consensus begins speaking: "We will guide from the inside of each of you, gently and in a familiar way. Everything here will feel familiar. We would like you to feel into the energy coursing through your body in this moment. Without any stories, we're simply feeling all the various directions, feeling the currents of energy in various places in the body; some in a more obvious flow than others. We're just letting our awareness focus on the energy within. Now we will draw your attention into the being of all of this energy that you feel coursing. You are AS all of the energy that you feel coursing.

"We would like to invite you now to imagine any teacher throughout all of history. Male, female, religious, non-religious, it does not matter. Just hold that teacher in your mind for a moment. Now, direct your attention once again to being AS the energy that's coursing in your body. We're going to take a nice deep breath in and when we do, we want you to breathe in the presence of the teacher that you have in your imagination. On the count of three: One. Two. Three. Breathe in. As you breathe out, breathe that teacher all throughout the body.

"Now, leave your entire awareness completely open. Become aware once again of the energy coursing in your body. Direct your awareness into that energy AS that energy. The energy of your teacher. You as teacher. Teacher as you.

"In the body as teacher, let us look at the quality of thoughts in relationship to self here. See whether there are any stories. Notice what the foundations of any stories are, if they are even present. Look at the range of things that are — or are not — present. Notice if you have any expectations. Any disappointments. Any surprises. And then any stories around these things. In any story you have, recognize relationship to past. Recognize the historical context of any stories. Look at all the dynamics at play. Simply being aware of yourself as the teacher, teacher as you.

"Now, from this vantage point you can recognize all the complexities of the mind that either have been at play or are at play in the moment. You can see how very hard your mind has worked to keep you safe. These various thoughts have been working diligently to keep you in a certain way of life. A certain *safe* way of life. We can look at all of that work of the mind by pulling back a little bit and looking at it objectively in a genuine state of wonder, through the eyes of the teacher. The teacher sees the mind in a genuine state of fascination, of curiosity. And as we bring in energies of wonder and fascination and curiosity we can feel an opening in the field. You can feel an opening in the energies. We can feel things beginning to soften. There's no effort that we have to put out here. It is simply the way that we are casting our awareness. As things continue to relax and soften, the clouds of these stories begin to dissolve. We can feel the presence of the purity of truth.

"Feeling into that truth, we're going to take a nice deep breath in through the third chakra, at the solar plexus. We're going to intentionally focus on wonder, fascination and curiosity, and then we're going to exhale that out through our heart into the collective. So take a nice deep breath in through the third chakra. Focus on wonder, fascination, and curiosity, and we're going to breathe that out through the heart into the collective. We can feel the aliveness in the presence of our teacher here within.

"We're going to do that again, and as we do we're going to recognize that it is the teacher breathing out this presence into the collective. Take a nice deep breath in through the third chakra. Wonder and curiosity and fascination . . . and out into the collective.

"The more we do this exercise the more discerning we can become, not only to the presence of teacher as me in the moment, but the living of teacher as me. The living of teacher in everyday life. That which speaks, speaks as teacher. That which walks, walks as teacher. That which listens, listens as teacher. That which sees, sees as teacher. That which is doing the exercise aware of the quality of thoughts, as teacher.

"We will remind you that every time this exercise is done, you are calling teacher into collective awareness, into your awareness, into your field, into the field of those around you. As you can see, this is a beautiful time for the presence of all teachers to be here in this realm. It is a beautiful time for humanity to be in the company of all teachers.

"Now, the mind will have a tendency to feel great burden here, to feel great responsibility and a need to get things right. We can assure you there is nothing to get right. This is all about allowing the presence of the teacher to be here. You have choice, and all choices will be honored. We are all available. We are all enthusiastically excited to be in your company. And we will be happy to answer any questions you may have at this time before we yield."

Question from participant: "Will the presence of teachers make it more possible for me to fulfill my life's purpose?"

Consensus: "It is not that you will be able to, you are able to. And you're doing so perfectly. This is where the mind can feel very burdened in its sense of responsibility. You're already doing what you came here to do. You're already willing. You do it in the decisions that you make about your work. You do it in the decisions that you make about what to create. You do it in the decisions about how late to sleep. There is no right formula for this.

"All of the teachers integrating into this reality are you as well. It feels chaotic to a human mind because a mind is used to a rhythm of routine and control. And that routine and control has a certain energetic familiarity and comfort in its zone. Without the familiarity of that rhythm, of that comfort zone, it can begin to feel overwhelming to feel all that you're feeling. The presence of teacher as you can show you, doing the exercise with self as teacher, where the stories are contributing to the sense of burden: what you thought it would feel like; what you're supposed to be doing; what you think about; your sense of worth. These are all tied to historical things about what happens if you don't get it right; about being worthy; about being inadequate. All of these old things. You see all of this when you truly embody the presence of the teacher. The teacher that throughout all of history has been present only because it was here to guide. And it was only able to be here to guide because of its purity of being; it's purity of acceptance of all that is and the acceptance of the chaotic feeling: Woohoo, there's a lot going on here!

"The teacher is the purity of love for all that's underway, all that is transforming, all that is already transformed, all that is still to be seen in the transformation process. So it is a glorious experience for all teachers to be here in your company and to be part of this process. You are doing it perfectly. *We* are doing it perfectly. Have fun with the sense of chaos. Fall to the floor on a day that you feel overwhelmed. You will not be stuck there. It's just a feeling that's needing to be expressed and seen and cared for. The purity of love that is brought to each and every single one of these feelings, these thoughts, these relationships, these moments, these events, these "other" people, these expectations, these things from the past coming into the present . . . all of it is perfect. You've heard this many, many, many, many times. And now the invitation is to live this. To live that wonder. To live the feeling of magnificence in the scale of all that's possible and all that we're experiencing. With wild abandon and embrace, we welcome all that you experience. We experience it with you. Now you get to experience all of it as us. Us as you."

Question from participant: I know all of this is serious, but it also feels really . . . fun?

Consensus: "This is fun. We said early on that we are not playing. By that we simply mean this isn't a game in which once you complete your goal, you're finished. That's not what's happening here. This isn't an imaginary thing. This is a very real experience. This is a very real, transcendent experience that we're in together. Sometimes the enormity, which is a story in and of itself, feels too much. To the mind, the human experience of the enormity of scale of all that's going on, and the possibility that we can be communing with non-physical entities, is a little too far to go until there is a lived experience that tells the truth.

Our aim here is to inspire, in a visceral way, the lived experience of what's really true. What's really possible. And this, my friends, is just a glimpse into your capabilities, into *our* capabilities.

"As we have crept in through little energetic crevices, many of you have seen your metaphysical abilities opening up. Understandings opening up. New ways of seeing life overall and your own life, opening up, opening up, opening up. Imagine all of this now with the full presence of all of us. Count on that. Embody that. As you do this exercise have that trust. Have that level of faith. Have that level of knowing. Have the level of clarity that is possible. A genuine, genuine, genuine, presence as teacher. Look at how phenomenal that anchor is for the new. Look at what a gift for humanity that is. Do you see what we've been doing?

"All of these "teachers" are representations of All That Is in its intention to be of service to humanity. This lives through us.

"We will remind you to call on us frequently. Call on any of us. Call on all of us. Have fun with this exercise. We will remind you of the layers of benefit to this exercise. It will shift every single time you do it. We're here with you. We are here as you, as things come up. That's the whole intention. You can do this exercise as you walk. As you shower. As you pray. As you sit down and do it with great intention. As you're cooking. As you're dialing. As you're cleaning. We will remind you again that the point of this exercise is this *visceral* state of being. The mind will have a tendency to want to control this, to keep it in the head. That is not effective at all. In the head is where you've been.

That is where humanity has been for all this time. The answer to the call for love that has been happening for eons within humanity is here in the visceral state. So answer that call. Again and again and again and again, allow yourself to viscerally *be* the presence of that answer. We thank you for the opportunity to be here with you."

The sky proposed
to me tonight
in star diamonds

This happens each night, of course,
to any heart who will notice it.

Sometimes we miss the moves
the beauty of this Universe
is always trying to put on us.

TWENTY-THREE

WE ARE: CONSTELLATION

After myriad ways of practicing how to invite and experience the Divine teachers within, Consensus shifted me and the group to an entirely new level of engaging with them: collective channeling . . .

Before we have even entered into the meditation state, Consensus begins narrating: "Tonight is very much about yielding. We use this word intentionally and we are intentionally not saying a great deal about what we are coming into. That will engage the curiosity of the mind and create a sense of nervousness or expectation, even fear. So, once again we will say the word for tonight is: yielding. You may think of this in many ways, the easiest is to perhaps just to imagine taking a back seat in your vessel to go on this experience together. Let the mind simply ease into the back and become witness.

"As we let that mind begin to yield, our thoughts drifting away, we begin to feel our bodies settling. We need be no further than right here, right now. We are present with you to assist in the relaxation; to be part of the energies of relaxation with you. So, we'll just ask you to invite us in to the intention of relaxation. There's no effort here. Anything that would normally be efforting is now sitting in the back seat just observing. You do not need to know where we are going, you do not need to know the way. We are happily taking care of all logistics.

"Now, in your normal gatherings you would at this point speak of your intention to be of service. That intention remains tonight, but we are as service *together*. Do you understand this? We are as service itself to that which is in the highest interest of all. It can be no other way. This gathering is to allow the service to be done in the way that it is directed from on high, if you will. Divine service, divinely guided. Simply be in the yielded state to allow everything that is happening here to happen through you. A door that is standing wide open does not need to direct the flow of what comes through, it simply needs to be open.

"We invite you to realize the flow that is happening through you, including the flow of these very words. As you receive these words you receive the energy that is flowing with these words; the energy upon which the words are flowing. Do you understand? This energy is happening through you because *we* are happening through you. You and this field of consciousness we all share are the arena. You are the structure in which this transmission is taking place.

"Now, understand that as the arena, as the structure through which all of this is flowing, the energy of Consensus — the Divine guidance, the Divine entities — is happening within you. The state of union is flowing through you, as you. You are accustomed to thinking of Consensus as an "other" with which you engaged or united. When we have previously invited you into the arena to be with Consensus that has been a language we needed to use to work with the mind so as not to incite fear. We are at a stage now where there is an invitation to have this experience in a united state, consistently.

"We will remind you that this is a multi-dimensional experience. It is happening on many levels, most of which are beyond your recognition or even comprehension, for we are not just of service to a single dimension or two dimensions or even three dimensions. We are in service to all dimensions. The impact of your intention, or *our* intention, is incredible.

"Now, in recent gatherings you have had an opportunity to open the energetic field in a very particular way, and it was that 'work' that is allowing this experience in this moment. Understand, please, that as all of you, as *we,* allow this experience here in this way we are setting up this potential, this capability, within the collective. We are creating a template, if you will, that is not unlike what you might call a constellation for collective channeling, a group channeling vessel. To become a group vessel, this field — *we* — are the arena in which this transmission is taking place.

"This is new, yes. And this is the potential we have been easing you into. You may have noticed recently an increase in the intensity of our gatherings, a momentum building in order to propel you into this capability. In this moment we simply ask you in your yielded state to let the breath of Divine presence flow through you, flowing through this arena, if you will, unimpeded. Let everything take root and calibrate to the group experience, to the collective experience, imprinting this potential as the template here.

"Now, we have used the language of the idea of collective channeling, or group channeling. This does not mean that every voice will be the vocal message that is transmitted. Some may be the echo that furthers the reverberation throughout. Some may be the lift. Some may be the deepening. There are many aspects to a transmission. You may think of it as a song with many notes. There is a singer. There are the instruments for notes played. There are microphones. You get the idea.

"Now, in this time many people have the energy of Christ in mind. When there is the speaking of Christ's resurrection, it has never been that there would be resurrection of a single individual. It is not Jesus the man being resurrected. It is the Christ consciousness, the consciousness of Christ itself. That means this awakening, this resurrecting happening throughout humanity, is a collective experience. It is happening through individual vessels, yes, but furthered through the collective experiences as is happening in this very moment. Humanity will begin to collectively experience Christ. So when we consider what is flowing throughout this arena in this moment, it is very much the heralding of Christ; the heralding of the moment of resurrection.

"Understand, friends, you do not need to rise to the occasion. All are lifted in this experience. This is a prime example of the end of effort. When you simply surrender to the lift. Every stage of this awakening has been part of a process. This will continue to be a process, and it is necessary and important to allow for the integration of these energies, for the shifting and the reorientation to an entire new way of being. We must do so without rushing the process, without overwhelming the mind that will try to jump in and figure it out, have some kind of control or impulse to be afraid of what is underway. This is intentionally a compassionate process for the mind. We will not rush, but we will also not deny. This *is* underway. This *is* happening. This *will* continue. And we will be in compassionate, kind service to all aspects of being.

"This is, in fact, a new template for being that we are establishing in this gathering. We will continue to work through this template going forward, as we move into more and more union and come together in this way you will find it easier and easier to release the pains of the separation consciousness and separation identity — the only place where all of that pain is so widely held. As we all lift together, there is a natural release of that which was holding us down. Everything in this way knows freedom.

"You will notice the key that unlocked this very door to freedom in this gathering was the word 'yielding.' When we allow the part that has previously been in control to yield, simply to get in the back seat for the journey, that which is yielding gets the benefits of the freedom as well — without any of the effort, without any of the struggle. Other language used around this has been 'surrender, 'allowing, 'receiving.' All true, all true. The idea of yielding says to the mind: you are still present; you may still be here, simply in the back seat, still along for the ride. You need not stand in front of the door and monitor what is trying to come through. You need not monitor, you need not analyze, you need not check to make sure that they have the hall pass. You are now entering a stage of not only being taken care of Divinely, but being part of what is, collectively, Divine caretaking.

"You have an idea in this gathering of how we will work together going forward. What is ahead for us is a powerful new beginning, if you will. It is indicative of the momentum, the acceleration that is underway and that will only continue to increase. We will take everything at a pace that allows everyone to remain steady and stable as much as can be through this incredible time of change, while also catalyzing ever more union, resurrection, awakening.

"There is much more to come in our work together, our work as one, our work *as* service, and we look forward to that. We will end this session tonight on a note of sincere and profound gratitude for all that is made possible by your willingness. As a reminder, none of you have the manual. We are creating the manual itself — we *are* the manual — as we go along. So, there is no need to try to anticipate, to figure out, to remember, to map it all out. That is pointless. That is engaging the mind in an analysis of this process, and that is fruitless. This is so far beyond the mind. We are, in fact, engaging so intently multi-dimensionally here that you may begin to experience in deeply restful states much more information as time goes on because we are pulling the information that is available in other dimensions into your awareness here. As we all come together, multiple dimensions are becoming more and more available. And we will be assisting in the coming months and years with resources to assist in the integration of that new understanding. Those are new perspectives, new-to-you information, if you will, as you continue to evolve and reorient again and again and again.

"We say again: this *is* happening. We *are* in this together. It is our great, great joy. Thank you for all you are allowing at this time in union. Thank you for this gathering and for this love."

I am not a poor
hungry thing
here to beg
for crusts of light

This life is no
arranged marriage
to darkness

I am pulling the veil
off the thousand suns
in my chest.

TWENTY-FOUR

THE TIME HAS COME

I was shown that it is time for all of us now to "come out" to our True Self when I was awakened one morning from a deep sleep with a powerful call to sit up and receive the following message: THE TIME HAS COME . . .

Here I see a veil around Earth lift and the "air" clear for all, then the message continues:

"For those who Know – those whose light will become visible to others – you have a responsibility now. Speak only your Truth of Love and nothing more (meaning do not embellish and trust your ability to speak from your higher Self). This is very important, for this is the integrity of Light."

Here I see the "leaving behind" of many outdated physical/mental/emotional bodies and new forms take their place, then the message continues:

"You are the Way. Understand with all your being that you Know this and the Way will be seen by others. Others will then awaken to their own choices."

I watch now as a massive gathering of countless Divine beings – masters, archangels, angels, etc. – come together throughout the cosmos. They all watch in jubilant celebration as individual bodies of light begin to illuminate one by one around planet Earth.

I say it's time to realize
that we hold a sloshing
amount of light
in the cup of each cell
and some Divine Party Animal within
continues to raise us
like a glass of joy
in a toast of celebration
to the wonder of being—
Cheers!

TWENTY-FIVE

READY TO FLY

The "TIME HAS COME" message was reiterated to me later when I was in a strange place between a dream and a vision. I was not asleep but I was also not awake . . .

I approach a large cement circle with a fire pit in the center where a large golden fire is burning. In the upper left corner from where I sit, a golden bridge appears and Buddha walks across and sits down on a bench in front of the fire. Another bridge forms in the upper right corner and Jesus walks across and sits down. Shortly many bridges form and others gather round, though they are quite faint and I cannot make them out clearly.

Shortly, a strong elderly Native American chief approaches from the other side of Jesus, bends over and knocks his tomahawk onto the cement several times until it breaks. This is to signify peace, ridding the present moment of any past reputations. The chief then turns and walks away.

Next comes Pope Francis, looking old and rather haggard from carrying a load too heavy to bear. He takes out his Bible and knocks it repeatedly against the cement until the upper half of the book breaks off. He keeps hold of the remaining bottom half, though still not happy with it, and walks away.

Next comes a very elderly man dressed all in white. He is being helped to the circle by two winged angels, also in white. I understand this is Father Time. When he approaches the circle he takes off his glasses, puts them on the cement by the fire, and steps on them, smashing them to little pieces. He no longer needs to see time. He then walks all the way around the circle, still aided by the angels but much sturdier, and then walks away.

Buddha and Jesus are still gathered here, as am I. We all come to the edge of the circle, bend down and silently pray. Shortly, Buddha stands up and takes off his *khata* (ceremonial scarf) and drops it in the same place where the others have broken their items. He is ridding himself of old ritual, which serves no purpose now.

Jesus then takes off his sandals and places them with Buddha's khata. He does this to indicate that we no longer need to walk this long road. We are ready to fly.

PART THREE

WHAT WE ARE WAKING UP INTO

THINGS ARE ABOUT TO GET INTERESTING

Things are about to get interesting.
The more you open
to the light of the Wild Sun
the more motivated She'll be
to pour her golden drink upon you.

You think your life was crazy now?
Just wait until you let love in!
You think She'll bring a sip of holy wine
to your lips,
but She'll pop the cork right off
this world
and intoxicate all existence!

Surround yourself with people
who have already been brave enough
to yank their souls
from the straight jackets
of their buds
and let the blossom
of their freak flags fly—
you will need this encouragement.

Because things are about to get interesting.
What used to be your reverent postures
will madly start trying
to pull God
into your body.

All your grounded words
will turn into swooping birds
of unpredictable poetry
and all your polite ways
will become true
maniacs for love.

Are you sure you're ready
to turn your respectable life
into a wild parade?

Perhaps consider this
before you pray like that
again.

TWENTY-SIX

END OF HELL

As mentioned previously, our awakening momentum is as much a creative process as it is a destructive one. Both of these aspects of transformation contribute to the confusion and mayhem inherent in large-scale change. While this confusion and mayhem will continue and even intensify for some as our fear-based consciousness doubles down on its effort to survive, we will, in fact, soon begin to realize a reality far easier than what we have ever known before. And that reality will be known in large part by all that is ending.

Over the years I have experienced many large-scale endings in the ethereal energetic fields that are making their way into the incarnate field of humanity. It is like I encounter stars whose bright lights are still a few years from arriving in our awareness, and when that light finally reaches all of us we will realize that its glow will now always occupy places where darkness used to be. One of the most profound and emotional "ending" experiences I have had began when, in a meditation with Corene, I suddenly entered a realm that would traditionally be considered hell . . .

The feeling here is solely an alignment with the archetypal representation of the realm of hell; there is no pain, no fear, none of that. I am simply to understand the presence of this realm.

Before me are black-cloaked beings with their backs to me lined up on risers like a choir. They are all reaching out for something. There is a palpable feel of a healing potential present in this moment and every being here is seeking something in anticipation. The beings begin to stomp their feet in revolt. They will no longer be patient. They demand the healing. This is their revolutionary moment.

Shortly, a red-cloaked being, the classic archetype of the devil, appears in the back of the room holding a scepter. He walks up through a middle passageway dividing the risers, stops at the front of the room, then turns to face the black-cloaked beings with his scepter raised. After a moment the devil slams the scepter down with a powerful thud and says, "The time has come." He closes his eyes and surrenders.

Instantly, every single black-cloaked being in the risers melts and disappears. I feel a *massive* swell of relief rise up within all of humanity, and I become overwhelmed, heaving tears.

Through my tears I see what happens next and utter, "Oh my God." I watch in shock as the color begins to drain from the devil's red cloak and from the devil himself. His entire being shifts into a blend of luxurious colors that get brighter and lighter, brighter and lighter, until finally everything is exquisite transparent light. Now, where the archetype of the devil once stood there is only the presence of God.

I look around me, and the entire space has changed. The risers are gone and there is simply a vast, empty room. It is not as though the risers or black-cloaked characters or the devil will be replaced by something else; the entire space becomes an abandoned space that is no longer needed. The realm of hell is no longer needed. The very *idea* of hell is no longer needed.

I am filled with deep emotion as the experience ends because I am fully embodied with what is in store for humanity. Afterwards, still in tears, I say to Corene, "It is a shame I can't share with the world the feeling of dissolving the realm of hell, or the experience of witnessing the dissolution of the devil to reveal God. The world would heal in an instant. All the ancient beliefs tethered to the idea or philosophy of hell would dissolve in an instant."

Darling, bottom line, we're all beautifully
animated dust
and to make any kind of hierarchy
comparing dust to dust
seems rather silly,
does it not?

TWENTY-SEVEN

END OF ANCIENT ELDERS

A deeply "ancient" kind of ending came while I was in the arena harmonizing with Consensus. Every gathering with them is different, but this moment felt particularly powerful, almost reverential . . .

The collective vibration throughout the arena grows still save for the slow rise of what feels like the echo of a continuous one-note baritone chant from deep within some kind of cosmic chamber. The chant is coming from countless ancient wise elders. This is a distinctly masculine kind of gathering, representing the masculine intention of wisdom from the elders' perspective. Words like 'Sanskrit' and 'Native American' come up among the ancients, noting varying kinds of ancient wisdom voices. The harmonizing rising up through this deep echoing chamber flows out into the arena, and out into the collective field. Within my body I feel a pulsing, like a drumbeat. It feels ceremonial, and it aids everyone in humanity in their ability to harmonize.

Palpably present here now is a fantastic combination of profoundly deep sorrow, grief and compassion mixed with the intentions of truth. These intentions of truth have a very tender foundation.

The energies of these wise elders are connecting to part of the Divine that was always inherent in this reality — teachings of the purity of Divine Love that were passed into this reality. This truth, this compassion, this purity of Love has always been embedded within everything, and lives within these wise elders.

I see now a foundation that looks like pillows, soft and tender, so pure in Love. Stacked upon these soft, tender, gentle pillows of foundation are what appear to be generations of children that are lost, who have remained lost throughout history, and have had no interest in these foundations of truth. And these generations of lost children have begat generations of lost children that begat generations of lost children, and so on. So, the longer humanity has continued to populate, the further away from these tender truths humanity has become. But all the while, this collection of wise elders has never moved. They have always remained.

The pulsing drumbeat that brings all beings into the same tempo is very much like a heartbeat. The heartbeat of humanity. In this heartbeat there is an owning up to all suffering bequeathed through the traditional male presence, through patterns of domination, conflict and control. And in that owning up, there is a recognition that within every one of these inherited patterns, every one of the beings that holds these "male" energies, including *all* humans, there is also foundational wisdom present. Within what we have called throughout history "male" energies, there has always been this foundational wisdom in energies referred to as "feminine." In truth, the energy of foundational wisdom is neither male nor female. There is simply a lineage that begat the fear-based, dominating, conquering energies, and within that lineage there has always been this healing foundational wisdom that has been repressed and latent.

All of these wise elders are now, and have always been, holding the truth of history and humanity's collective regret in compassion. They hold all of it now, and are taking responsibility for both the paths that humanity has taken in the past and the path humanity is on now.

In this moment, in this ceremonial setting, they all put down their instruments. The instruments of war. The instruments of teaching. It appears like an infinite line of ancient wise elders, all of them setting down their instruments. In some cases it is a robe. In some cases it is a book, a staff, and so on.

My body now fills with emotion. Having put all their instruments down, all the ancient elders bow down and touch their foreheads to the earth. They become neither master nor student, but simply at one with the wisdom of the Earth, Earth being the home of humanity. I can see within me an entire cosmos living within planet Earth.

Now, there is no more need for a "wise elder." There is no more need for the idea of anything "ancient" because the wisdom has been given over; it has been released from all history, ideas of history, completely into the now. In doing so, there is a release of the idea of masculine and feminine energies, the idea of elder, the idea of wisdom itself and any of the ancient lineages of wisdom so that it all becomes simply the Truth that is.

What the wise elders are doing in this moment is akin to untying the base. They are releasing themselves as the base to which the history of masculine and feminine ideas were tethered. Again, the line of these wise elders is extremely long and there is complete agreement among all of them. In this agreement I watch the cosmos around Earth and the cosmos within Earth unite. All of the wise elders dissolve into the greater collective field. They release themselves and the ideas of their conceptual history into the entire cosmos of God.

I am woven
of a light
that knows no
exclusion
or opposite

and my dear joy,
I have arrived in you.
I am fully yours.

TWENTY-EIGHT

END OF OPPOSING SIDES

Another ending related to "male" energies was revealed in a weekly gathering with Consensus and my community. It began as I stood at the top of the arena and watched the thousands of light beings that make up Consensus enter in a lively, chaotic manner. They gradually settled down to harmonize with each other until they became one multidimensional "note" that I would translate. I could feel the immense love and joy they were experiencing in this gathering as they began to speak through me . . .

"We are in this moment anchoring into Mary's field more masculine energy. The reason why, of all things, masculine energy is so that this energy can experience the level of joy that is possible without any particular kind of force accompanying it, or any kind of earned state of joy. In this way, there is a softening of the masculine energy. In this way there is a neutralizing even of the concept of male and female, masculine and feminine energies, which is part of the intention of this action. Joy is simply joy. We do away with the masculine and feminine titles or labels, and we simply have joy that can pervade any kind of energy.

"This is part of the undoing of old patterns of recognitions of labeling. You can imagine that these are unbraiding patterns: labels and words, that we identify with various tendencies, behaviors, expectations, roles, etcetera.

As we unbraid these patterns we find that new relationships with everything is possible. The old relationships are no longer even seen; they're no longer visible or accessible. Relationships to past associations with behaviors or expectations based on masculine or feminine or any other kinds of labels — many, many, many different kinds of labels — will now begin to dissolve. They become irrelevant. They become not applicable to what is at hand.

"Remember that the exploration now is in a *unitive* state. What is the union of masculine and feminine? It is neither masculine nor feminine, it is a union of both. The union of what would previously be considered opposites, is now felt as both a neutral pattern or neutral experience, but also one of unusual and unrecognized joy because we have not experienced this pattern previously. It's like discovering a new species that is within all species; a new life that is within all of life.

"This is the reason why, prior to this gathering, we assisted in a clearing of Mary's second chakra, clearing old paradigms of gender, associations with gender, and the ancient lineages so deeply entrenched in identity of masculine and feminine.

"This neutralizing pallet of humanity now is the next wave of awakening. We will do well not to speak of things in terms of masculine and feminine energies but simply to call it love. The expression of love without taking a side of any kind, without taking an opposite stance of any kind, an opposing reflection of any kind. It is love reflecting love. It is love recognizing love. It is love awakening to love."

It turns out your willpower,
all that efforting,
is astoundingly weak
compared to the easeful way
beauty shares herself
through the form of a hummingbird.

TWENTY-NINE

END OF EFFORT

I have repeatedly been shown that effort — the constant striving to achieve, to figure things out, to get it all done — is one of the key things that is coming to an end. Consensus confirmed this in a blessedly lighthearted way during a gathering with my private community. Before the session started, the mood among participants in my community was noticeably lively and upbeat. There was a joviality present without apparent cause; it was not a special occasion or a notable date. When we went into meditation together and I entered into the arena, the energy within Consensus was noisy and exuberant . . .

"We have a very large gathering here this evening. The enthusiasm that was brought to the fore in the beginning of this gathering was due in part to the enthusiasm of this arena full of wise beings. It has the feel of an exciting match that we're all watching, an event in the arena that is electrifying. The match is exciting because there are no losers. Part of the fun of watching this from our perspective in the stands is that so many of the players do not realize that there are no losers. This is a game of all winning.

"The excitement comes also from the fact that, in actuality, the game is already over; everyone has already won. Now it is simply a matter of coming into the realization of that fact, basically transitioning from the field to the stands with us. We are in this context very much the cheerleaders, and we really like this role. Can you imagine *wise* cheerleaders? We've said 'wise' so articulately, so clearly here in jest. That's not to say there isn't wisdom in cheerleading; there's immense joy in cheerleading and joy is always wise. Why? Because it is tied to, and part of, our innate nature. That is the truth of our nature, the truth of *your* nature, the truth of *Our* Divine nature. So, we are experiencing and enlivening that joy for ourselves and for you, infusing this field in this moment with that same joy, that same cheerleading.

"We are taking a brief pause in this moment for Mary. She is in this moment, in her body, sensing a feeling that this cheerleading for this present stage of awakening has come up from deep, deep, deep, within her like an ancient journey that has finally reached this destination. So, we are in this moment catching everything up to this stage in the body vessel.

"It can feel very intense to bring along what some would call the darkness of the past. It can feel heavy — that history, that lineage, that remembrance, that holding on to things that felt like suffering. It can feel intense, it can feel painful, it can feel nauseating at the various times as we bring those things into the light. But what feels uncomfortable in the body is that piece that feels like it is its responsibility to bring everything along. It is the piece of us that has lived in separation consciousness; the piece that has felt so burdened. That piece feels like it is the one that needs to bring along all that still has to be healed into the light. So in this moment in Mary's body vessel there is a recognition that that piece, the piece that feels burdened, that is holding what is basically anchored to all of that history, *need do nothing*. That is the whole point: it is the effort that stops now.

"Using the arena here in this moment, filled with light, you can see the game that is going on down on the field is the game of effort, and once that game of effort stops then all there is, is the light — the light that surrounds everything, that is within everything. Once the effort stops the eyes are open. This is what is happening on the field of humanity, facilitated recently in large part by fear. When the COVID-19 pandemic started and everybody had to come inside, everybody had to stop the effort on a massive scale. Many of you in this collective field tonight know the magnificent shifts and changes that began to occur right around that time and still continue today.

"Now, we, Consensus, are not a massive collective of Divine beings by accident. It's not that we didn't have anything else to do so we thought we would visit here — when we say "here" we mean this particular field, this particular gathering. This is very strategic. We are a large collective of Divine beings because of the enormity of what is underway in the world today with humanity, and as we have said previously, you are all anchors for the new. You are in the arena. There is a little bit of you still on the field, still yearning to wake up from the game. But there is so much more of you in the stands with us than there ever has been previously. In that way you can see how you enrich us as much as we enrich you.

"We are here with a continuum of feelings this evening, exuberant joy and excitement and eagerness, but that is not to diminish the scale of things that people still feel in their own day-to-day lives. Both are true. Both are here in this arena, both are here in this collective field, both are in each of you. But you all recognize that that balance is shifting more and more and more. So it is helpful to reflect, because as you reflect you have greater understanding, greater awareness and appreciation, but you also have greater curiosity. You are expanded, and the more you expand the more curious you get about what else is there of me, of us, of life, of love.

"We bring into the conversation this remembrance of what some experience as a struggle, that in our history and that which we're still wanting to heal, to encourage a reflection but also to encourage the understanding that the effort to heal can stop. It is simply being in the light. Being as an anchor of light is in and of itself the healing, not only for you but for others. So, as you have experiences where you have an awareness of things that still feel difficult and still feel the burden of the old, you may feel that in your body. These are manifestations of various symptoms in your mind, the manifestations or repeating of various patterns, habits, reactions, etcetera. But recognize in the moment which part of you is feeling that and you will see that it is the part that is still standing on the field playing the game of effort. You have a choice to come up into the stands at any time and feel that resonance of excitement and cheerleading. We highly recommend it.

"We tell you this in part to inspire understandings and reflections in this moment, but we also do so strategically in preparation for things that will be coming. This is an important opening by re-shifting you a bit. You might imagine sitting comfortably in a chair and we have just shifted you a bit to get you comfortable in a slightly different way.

"As you walk daily in the intention to be of service to yourself, to others, to the collective, and to all of us now, we would like to invite you to feel yourselves in the stands of the arena with us. Imagine scootching between us, making yourself at home. You know us, you're happy to see us, you know the cheers in the same way we do. We invite you to feel that power, feel that light, feel that enthusiasm, feel that joy. Feel it throughout your entire body. Feel the buzz of that resonance. Now imagine magnifying the luminosity of this arena exponentially. Magnify this sense of that radiance that you are a part of. It has been an absolute joy to embrace this field tonight, to be in your company, to be invited in with such warmth and trust and welcome. We thank you for this gathering. We thank you for this love."

Here's to those who refuse to stop
bringing forth the balm of their precious light
to the thirsty lips of the world.

THIRTY

END OF CONQUERING GAME

Related to both the end of opposing sides and the end of the game of effort, one morning I woke from a deep sleep being pulled into a simple paradigm shift that will have a massive influence on the world . . .

I travel with humanity in a progression from competition to collaboration, from "my life" to "all of life" consciousness, and from narrow role playing to vast exploration of our human potential. All of this is transpiring as I embody a new model of how we play games.

We develop games where the objective is to help the other person or team win. The goal is twofold: creativity, and depth of impact for others. We use our individual and collective skills, intellect and imagination. Everyone can play, and no one can lose.

We also develop games that have multiple objective decision trees. Each decision shows varying paths that reflect the potential for individual experience and collective impact. One can thereby explore evermore possibilities of life at micro and/or macro levels. Decisions that limit personal or collective growth lead to a stage where alternative decisions must be made in order to advance. The more one discovers the greatest potential for individuals and the collective, the more points one wins.

These games change not just our motivation but our way of thinking. They spark our curiosity to *be* differently, thereby creating a different world as they illuminate and reward recognition of our interconnectedness. They dramatically alter our ideas of success and purpose, making obsolete the old conquering, good-trumps-bad models of entertainment, education, governance, and spirituality. They break the cycle of conditioned belief in limitation and set us free to explore *all* of who we are as possibility-filled individuals populating our everything-is-possible humanity.

Go forth, glorious
"too much" ones
and pour your rivers of light
that quench the world.

Go forth and feed
every ravenous soul
from the generous table
of your heart
knowing your essence is one of feast,
not famine.

THIRTY-ONE

END OF INADEQUACY

At times when the momentum of my awakening intensifies or what I feel in the collective energies intensifies (inevitably there is a connection), I can always feel it in my body. This is not surprising given that the body is the vessel through which everything is processing. In one particularly intense stage, I had severe stomach pains for two weeks along with a clear sense that deep wisdom was trying to rise up but couldn't come through on its own. I asked Corene for help to explore what was happening and we scheduled a time to meet the next day. Twelve hours before our session, I passed out from the pain. I woke up two hours later still in pain but feeling "open" and ready to go into a deep meditative state with Corene. I was well aware this was going to be a doozy of an experience . . .

As we begin to settle into the session, I feel compelled to focus on just one question: What is the deepest desire of my higher Self?

Shortly, I enter into a realm that at first appears to be empty, but the sense of vastness is distinctly palpable. It feels like the scale of what is to be integrated in my own life and into humanity, and it is enormous. The enormity is not overwhelming, it's just an adjustment. And this adjustment is part of the lesson.

A vast ocean opens up in my awareness, and on the shore at the water's edge are small buckets sitting upright in the sand. The ocean feels like the scale of God, and in each bucket I feel a profound yearning to experience the Oneness of the ocean of God in their little containers. Simultaneously, in each bucket is a profound sense of unworthiness, and a woeful feeling of inadequacy and inability to take in such scale as the ocean of God.

I can feel my own history tied to the buckets' unworthiness and inadequacy, like a tethering to old stories and beliefs I have carried within my own sense of self since childhood: that I wasn't "enough." Deep in my human identity I believed I wasn't smart enough, capable enough, trained enough, big enough, etcetera. No matter how successful or secure, in the background of my life there was always a feeling of overwhelm and inadequacy.

As I recognize this old pattern within me, my awareness expands to encompass all of humanity and I see the same mindset. I see the collective become like a child that is insecure because it believes it is insufficient and unworthy, and it feels greatly intimidated and inadequate in the presence of great spiritual figures such as, for example, Jesus. That juxtaposition of inadequacy in the presence of power — even in the *idea* of the presence of power — lives in the foundation of humanity's consciousness. The collective has a pervasive consciousness of inadequacy in a global population of people who have been conditioned in countless ways to look outside of themselves and think they are not as good as others in the world. Humanity itself is like a mirror of inadequate consciousness.

Watching how we try to manage through life in our inadequacy, I see humans constantly making small efforts, mostly in ways to comfort themselves but not in ways to rise to their full potential. And I see that this at the root of all relationships with the world at large. In a good-trumps-bad paradigm, the "good" constantly strives to feel better, so in its conquering way the good is trying to make the inadequate piece feel better. That inadequate part has no concept of being truly adequate, so it does not understand its power. It does not have the capacity to understand because it is not in a consciousness of adequacy or power.

While I understand what is being shown to me, I don't understand what this has to do with the deepest desire of my higher Self. So, Corene makes the invitation for my higher Self to join this experience, to come in and sit in a chair with me.

After a moment, without any noticeable transition, I suddenly realize that I am every part of this experience at once: that which is speaking, that which is being spoken through, that which is being spoken about, and the "all" field within which everything is happening. I am not just channeling, I am the movement of what is being channeled and the field through which there is movement. I say, "We have to look at this experience differently. The whole point of *integration* is that there is not a separate chair. We are all here already. There is essentially no separation between the space that I'm in, 'me,' the asking, and that which I've asked for. It's all in the same being. This is where I Am."

The feeling in this moment is unique from any previous metaphysical event. It is an indescribable fullness and enlivened scale of being everything at once. I say, "I'm just in what Is. And everything is accessible from right here. Whatever the question, I'm going looking for wherever I Am. In previous experiences I have been in the primordial ground where there was an exquisite void of pure nothingness. The environment I am in now is a field of nothingness that contains everything. It is like the primordial ground that is filled. In the primordial ground I am aware of nothing and in this I'm aware of everything. It is not a cognitive awareness, though; it is a fullness of awareness more than minutely detailed cognitive awareness."

Corene asks, "Do you have a sense of how this is connected with the earlier experience of those enormous limiting beliefs that humanity has?"

Before me something akin to a kaleidoscope appears, and within it I can discern countless dimensions. I say, "You know how the fifth dimension may include the first, second, third and fourth dimensions, but the third dimension doesn't include the fifth? Well, now imagine the trillionth dimension contains all of the other dimensions. But the third dimension doesn't contain the trillionth. That's the scale of the canyon between what the third dimensional sense of inadequacy is and the capabilities of our greater consciousness."

Relating all of this back to the original question of what is the deepest desire of my higher Self, I continue, "When I say we are to know all that's in this canyon, I mean to *live as* all that's in this canyon."

I struggle to articulate what I am both perceiving and understanding. I say, "There's a reason why I can't do this in a way that is something *telling* me this, something illuminating things *to* me. This is the whole point: it needs to be an *integrative understanding*. ALL of "me" has to live this experience of moving into this canyon. This is not about just being told how it is, but experiencing the knowledge, experiencing the *movement through* that understanding of adequacy.

"This has to be done differently than it ever has before. This is not like any of the other experiences, it can't be like any of the other experiences. It's not going to be handed to me, that's the whole point. Now we are *together*. So in this united state, the understanding, the journeying, the movement, has to be in union. This is where we're at. Everything is now experiential in a much more unitive way. Not one piece over here to embody and experience and one piece over there to embody and experience, but we experience the canyon all together. It is becoming that which we are calling out for. Becoming the answer. This is about becoming that which we're crying out for, which includes the higher Self because it is the higher Self's calling that has brought itself now into union with this dimension.

"We have to understand that this whole process is different. The surrender is a different way. The surrender is to something much more *unitive*. And in that, we are no longer that which will be given something. We are becoming that which is given. This is a huge shift in our understanding, but the understanding, too, is part of shift. It won't come through the understanding of the mind and then the body. It's an understanding through this unitive consciousness because it is *becoming the understanding itself*. This is no longer something we're working out. This is something that we're *being*. This is not just the deepest desire of higher Self. It is the being of higher Self. It is the experience of *being* higher Self.

"In some ways this is so much easier and more encompassing, but it is a conceptual framework that doesn't work in third dimensional understanding. It doesn't work in a way of give and take, or give and receive. It doesn't work like that. We're past that now. Mary in particular is past that now. This is very important to understand, to approach in this way. Conveyance is the key. *Conveyance through being* is the key. Mary knew from the beginning she is the Message. She's not here to tell the message she is to *be* the Message. This is the *being* of the Message. The being of that which is being called into *BE*."

Corene asks, "So this is the new work?"

I start to correct her words, but Corene catches it first. "It's not work though, is it?"

"That's correct. This is the challenge. There isn't a conceptual framework to put this in. 'Work' implies that it's something to be done, something to figure out. And this is not it. This is the difference. This is entirely the difference. You see, in a mindset that says we can achieve if we're adequate enough to achieve, then we think we can figure this out or overcome barriers to it. This is not that idea. The idea of adequacy, overcoming, achieving, is the whole problem. That mindset leads us into a place where we are not meant to be now. It's not where we are . . . I don't even want to say 'going.' It's where we are arriving. Even that concept doesn't work because we are not moving towards something; we are moving *within* something — God-ness that is already here. It is like resting in all of the spaces between and within everything. We are simultaneously an answer to a question that we don't even have time to ask because we're already the answer.

"So, the revelation, the revelatory part of this process is developing the conveyance of *that*. This is Mary's presence. You don't have models or examples of this, so in that regard this is the modeling. I don't want to say this is the beginning of that process, it's more the entry into that space. It is completely different. All the beliefs just collapse. This is what's left when beliefs collapse. It's not the living of a new belief in a framework that our mind can understand. It's not that at all. It is living in the space beyond the old conceptual frameworks and being the conveyance of that. This is very specific to understand: *being the conveyance of that.*"

Corene is trying to take all of this in. "In being the conveyance of that, everything is dropping away?"

"You and Mary have spoken previously about the piercing of the soap bubble."

"Yes."

"What was in the soap bubble?"

Corene realizes the answer to her question is just the falling away of beliefs. She giggles and answers. "Nothing."

"Exactly," I continue. "The storytelling has had to happen in a way that people in the third dimension could understand it. It had to be these archetypal representations of place and person and story, events and laws and all of these sorts of things. Of course, perfectly fine and wonderful and beautiful and effective. And this was an exploration that we've all learned a great deal from — not just us but all dimensions have learned. Now, that exploration is moving in a different way. There will still be consciousness that explores in that way; there are still things to understand. But humanity's evolution as a whole is coming now into this space of developing the presence of True *being*.

"This expansive Self consciousness — All That Is, God, Love, Divine, Source, 'my' higher Self — this consciousness is entering into this present realm to develop the conveyance of *being Divine*. Do we know what that looks like? No. But Mary's presence here in this body, this thing that people can see, is an opening. It's like a portal. This portal travels around and little by little by little by little things come in and out, in and out, through this portal. Conveyance is happening on a completely different level than we realize it here now, and it will continue in that way as well as other ways. It will continue in the structure of the words, in new words, new energy with those words, new ways that the words are received and put together, and new energies with which those words are spoken or written or conveyed. But what people receive is the understanding upon which those words are coming. We don't have a conceptual framework to explain it at this time but it's coming.

"This integration has to happen in ways that it can be managed, for this vessel (Mary) to manage it, for others around to manage it, and for this vessel to find the right resources and community support to manage it in the same way that's happening right here in this moment. And all who support this transformation have to be able to manage what they're learning as well. So it's an integrating process. All of us together are doing this together. It's not just here, it's not just there, it's happening in infinite ways with infinite people as Mary moves through the world. Not just Mary, obviously, but she has a pivotal role."

At this point in the session I feel a distinct sense of ease in my stomach and say, "I feel a great sense of freedom in my stomach."

Corene replies, "Oh wonderful. So Mary's instincts were correct about the opening and the physical pain being a sign of something shifting?"

Focusing on the "instincts" part of Corene's question, I reply, "This is an example of separation language; we say there is some part that's telling us this thing, as opposed to *WE know*. Now we begin to claim ownership: *WE* have always known. The whole being has always known, so it isn't this part being told by that part, do you see? It's This Whole in the knowing. Certainly we can understand things in terms of Mary having a hunch or intuitively feeling, but we can begin to see that that framing in and of itself is a language of separation. We begin to *convey* things in a different way, and Mary in her speaking now will begin to be more cognizant of that. And in just that subtle way of conveying these things it will wake people up and allow that integration of Presence through new avenues, through these little windows.

"In countless ways our whole language framework has been around this, and we just take it for granted. It's the story way that we talk, it's how we have learned. Now, we will just tweak it, and in the most subtle ways that tweaking will have profound effects that people will have no idea about in the moment. They cannot be told directly, "This is you taking in things in a different way," because that is speaking to a consciousness that then tries to put things in a framework and understanding of the old ways. It can't be conveyed in that way. That's a step-by-step kind of way, the old way of puzzle-putting. That way is for the mind, and the new is not for the mind. The mind can't understand this because the mind is trained and structured in a different way, so as soon as we put things into that old structure we've lost where *All of It* really is. Divine information is present within and outside of the soap bubble. It is not within the design of the soap bubble.

"There is a deeply centering place Mary has realized. This is the individual portal, meaning you have it (Corene), somebody else has it, everyone has it through the individualized vessel. Unseen in this space is all Divine presence. Right now the reason why it is unseen by Mary is because Mary is part and parcel of it. So in this unitive consciousness there isn't a reason to need to see it as "other" in the old way. It's much more profound than that. It's much vaster than that.

"There needs to be the understanding that the assistance with some information for the individual vessel may still come around, but what's happening is on a much broader collective level. So, in Mary's experiences of Jesus, of Buddha, of light, of angels, of Archangel Michael, of soul groups, etcetera, all of those have been like looking through particular lenses. She could look at the vastness through a particular lens such as Christ consciousness, Buddha nature, the angelic light, etcetera. Where we are now in this unitive state is looking at everything without any lens. It is not actually looking at it, but *being it* without the need for lenses. So, the wisdom inherent in the Christ consciousness, the Buddha nature, the angelic realms, is already inherent in the being of this. There is no need to despair if there isn't the presence of luminous beings in one's experience because we are all realizing the luminosity of ourselves. It doesn't feel the same yet because we are integrating with the third dimensional beings. It's a process that just takes time. We have to let this vessel integrate and adjust to its luminosity and the collective field in which this vessel is existing and reflecting.

"We speak this as much for the integrative vessel (Mary) as for you, Corene, and so that this can be recorded to help us understand and remember that this is the process that we are in right now, and it looks differently. As much as this engagement with all energies, all consciousnesses, is changing, so too will the things that we think are the laws. Those laws were there to manage through the third dimensional lens, so the further we go in our integrating, the more we're able to develop the conveyance of things, we will come to realize that the laws change as well. And when I say change, I mean sort of fall away. They are simply recognized as not necessary anymore."

Corene asks, "Is one of those things that's falling away in this process the feeling of being disempowered?"

I reply, "Yes, which is at the core of the challenge. This is why Mary's work in particular is so focused on compassionately understanding pain. Because at the core of pain is where we are feeling our inadequacy, and the pain of separation bleeds through all of that consciousness. The compassionate understanding and approach to the source of pain is part of the seeping process of the integration. The more we can open our understanding compassionately to what has been our rejection of pain and the healing through the avenue of embrace, the more the opening of this integration can occur. This a really good avenue to work through in the third dimensional realm. It's so beautiful in part because it's effortless in a unitive state to do it, and people recognize that effortlessness. There's a relief in that effortlessness."

I don't want to go to any temple
I just want pillow talk
with God

THIRTY-TWO

END OF SEPARATION

While all of the "endings" I have experienced have been profound, perhaps the most significant was related to the origin of separation consciousness. Not surprisingly, it came during another palpably intense acceleration in both individual and collective energies. Corene and I were on a call together and we both noted that we had been feeling odd for several days. Additionally, I had been having a lot of pain in my sacrum after a particularly high-vibration gathering with my private community the previous week. There was a clear sense of some kind of momentum happening, but it felt somehow different from previous times of energetic acceleration. Corene said, "It feels like things almost align within me, but then don't stick. I'm frustrated by it, but also I just can't be bothered to be frustrated. It's weird."

"Yeah, something's definitely different," I say. "It feels like we're in the process of not just a deeper alignment but a *new kind* of alignment."

We agreed to do a meditation and ask for more information about what was happening . . .

As we relax into quiet and stillness, I begin to feel a tremendous ascending movement all around and within me, like a vast upward tsunami of energy. Inside this massive swell of energy I can see that my small separate "I" identity feels like a teeny tiny thing frantically trying to get oriented. It is very confused, unable to get its bearings inside the greater whole of "I Am" energies within which it is swirling. I feel a sweet mothering kind of compassion for it but cannot do anything to help stabilize it.

Unable to discern what to do, I ask Corene what she can sense in my field. After a moment she says, "Many things, but one of the first things is a feeling of the outer aspects of your body being stretched like a drum. There's so much space inside and there are all sorts of different energies contained within that space. The heart in particular is extremely open."

"This is in keeping with what I feel," I say.

Corene continues, "It feels like this is about the dissolution of physical boundary; addressing the belief that the physical self is separate from everything but there's a bursting through that veil now. The discomfort and pain you feel is related to resistance to this. There's a deeply primal fear here about loss of identity of self, as this body. This is not a conscious fear, it's more of a cellular fear." She pauses, then asks, "Can you hear what the fear is saying, what it's trying to express?"

I respond, "Ironically, what comes up with that fear at a very deep level is: 'I don't want to be here.' It feels like an echo down through my lineage. At the same time, it also feels like if this fear is not here then it's not loved. So, it's stuck in a contradiction."

I remember now an experience I had many years ago when I went into the memory of being in my mother's womb and felt extremely frustrated. I wanted out of the womb immediately. It felt too tight, and I was aggressively not okay being there. It wasn't that I wanted out into this

240

life, I just wanted out of that womb. Relaying this to Corene, I say, "It feels like that moment was significant in terms of how this fear I'm sensing now has been carried at the DNA level. If we think about it from my parents' perspective, neither parent wanted me to be here, so there was resentment, bitterness and anger in both sets of DNA. Then I, of course, carry that in my own body."

As I speak, I feel a painful increase in pressure in my sacrum. I continue, "This feels like trauma at a DNA level; the trauma of being unwanted and knowing it is true, so you don't want to be here. But I am very aware that the reason I *am* here is because I am the one to love all of these fearful energies. The reason these fearful energies didn't want to be here is because they didn't want to come here *again* and be unwanted."

Speaking these words, I now see what's playing out in humanity's awakening from the perspective of fear. I say, "Given that this is what's at the root of these old fearful energies, the very idea of transcending them goes right to the heart of their pain of being unwanted — being the thing that is left behind. If we think about the fear-based separation identity, this is the thing that's being transcended, so this all feels like it's a catch-22. To this old fear, transcendence feels like a rejection, and as has been shown many times, rejection is the very thing that gives separation its power. As long as there is the stronghold of feeling rejected at the DNA level, then there is the stronghold of the tether to separation identity. But it also feels like this is the last energetic knot tying us to that old separation paradigm."

As I'm saying all of this it feels like everything is opening up to be seen. The pain in my sacrum again intensifies. Deep within me I hear a yelling, "AAGHHH!" I have no idea what to do, so I ask us for Divine assistance and immediately an image appears. It is fear with a face that is very close so I can see it, but behind it I can see a very, very long tail stretching all the way back through history. On either side of the tail are Divine beings all the way down. This long chain of Divine beings on either side of the tail are here because this is not just the original energetic knot of fear tied to the old separation paradigm for me; this is the original knot that was tied to the *idea* of separation consciousness, period. I say, "We can't just attend to the fear at one level and then let all the other levels still remain. We can't do that. *I, Mary,* can't do that. Because my work is always about the origins."

Now my sacrum is on fire and I feel sick. As I'm feeling the pain, a scene opens up and I am shown that there is going to be a chain reaction of dissolution that starts the moment I face this fear, then it will continue all the way down through history, with all these Divine beings ensuring that it continues, continues, continues until it releases at the base. As the tail dissolves, all of the Divine beings will meld into one great big Presence right here in this earthly realm with me. So, where there was once fear there will now be only Divine Presence.

I focus on trying to sense internally any guidance on how to start this dissolution process, but nothing is there. Then I hear, "You are thinking in terms of doing, and that is the old way. You've asked for the guidance and now you just need to trust, because it is not you that has to do anything." As they tell me this, I see Divine Presence hold a mirror up very close to the face of the fear. The only thing in the mirror is love. I hear, "It is the Presence of Divine Love that does the 'action' so that the fear can see the truth." Over the next four minutes I watch as the chain reaction of dissolution starts in the face of the fear, and continues, continues, continues all the way down until it releases from the base. All the Divine Presence that has been assisting with the dissolution meld together and the whole space before me is Divine Presence. The separation paradigm is now nowhere in my awareness. I say in this moment, "It is done."

While the dissolution of fear was taking place, tensions repeatedly released in my sacrum. Now it feels wide open. I can't feel any fear, or any lineage of fear at all. I say, "This end of separation consciousness has happened in the same way the end of hell occurred. The cause has already happened, and soon the manifestation will be revealed. It's like a new star that is born and it will take some time for the light to reach our awareness."

We are intrepid enough
to set out
on the pilgrimage
toward this pearl
of limitless value,
toward these unspoken storehouses
of Grace
that restore us
with the most personal
and universal
intimacy
with our essence

THIRTY-THREE

IT IS ALREADY SO

There is this work, and all other work falls away: anything that arises in our awareness is already here. Accept it unconditionally for it is *already* God without condition. We will soon see it through God's eyes.

Anything that arises in our awareness is to be accepted as equal in value and potential to exist for it is *already* equally of God.

Anything that arises in our awareness is free to express what it is, as it is, for it is *already* God expressing freely.

Anything that arises in our awareness is to be embraced in the unity and Oneness with every other part of our being, for it is all *already* part of the Oneness that is God.

As we rise out of the dense darkness of separation consciousness to see the light, we remember: I AM as All Is: of God. There is nothing else. There is Cherishing Awareness being aware of and cherishing all there is to be aware of and cherish. We Are, All Is, *That*.

The belief that there is other than God is falling away. The stories born of this belief are falling away. God is reclaiming "our" story. God is telling Its own story. This is the story of Our return to awareness of Ourselves as unique aspects of God offering unique experiences to all aspects of God. It is so. It is so. It is already so.

Consensus has said many times that the invitation for all of us is to understand the depths of the beginning of the new. "We've spoken in the past about union with earth, humanity's home. We have said this is not just about planting new seeds; we are the new soil.

"As we are here at this new foundation in a unitive consciousness space, we are aware of the opportunity for every single step from this point to be into the new. We're aware that every single thought can be a thought into the new. Every single focus. Every single intention. Every single breath mind-fully, heart-fully, into the new. Every single thing that is encountered from this vantage point is encountered from a new perspective. The angle of perception is new.

"You can imagine looking at the world and its past through the five senses. What we can hear through our ears, what we can see through our eyes, what we can touch with our hands, etcetera. You might imagine that from the new perspective, the experience of the world is from the new capabilities to perceive. The easiest understanding of that is to see, and hear, and touch through the heart. What we read, we read through the heart. What we hear, we hear through the heart. In union with Divine beings our perception is that of the Divine vantage point.

"From the vantage point of unitive being, what is it that's being said in this moment? What is it that is being seen in this moment? What is it that is heard in the conversation that's happening in the moment? What is it that's seeing this relationship in the moment? What is it that's giving to the world in this moment? What is in relationship with life in this moment? Nothing that is known to the mind.

"The new is being created through visceral awareness. Everything that flows into the collective and from the collective, what is given and what is met, is done in visceral awareness. It takes out of the equation any mechanisms of control or expectation or need. You will enter into a period now that will feel to some confusing, to others boring, to others incredibly rich. Those who are confused or bored are hearing from their mind, because none of this is accessible viscerally to the mind. We will remind you that the compassionate viewpoint is that we are giving your mind, finally, a rest; a rest from all its burdens, from all its struggles, from all its weight. There's nothing that has to be *done* from this vantage point. This is a *being*.

"This shift is still a learning experience, and every moment is the lesson. Am I intending the new? Am I focusing on the new? Is this thought in the new?

"Literally, it is just a breath away. This is the path, and you create it as you step. Every single step, this is the path. You are standing on the new ground *as* the new ground. And every moment is the creation opportunity for the new."

MAKE YOUR LOVE VISIBLE

God had a great secret
that She couldn't keep

and one day
Her Heart exploded
with the Big Bang.

Her inability to contain Herself
became galaxies.

She poured Her Heart out and it slowly began
sorting itself out
into the Universe.

She spilled the beans (the stars)
so completely,
Her repressed blushing
became sunsets.

She whispered Her secret music
into the heart of every atom
and the electrons
could not help
but giddily dance.

All creation became a chatter box,
gossiping to each other nonstop
about the wild, loving mysteries
She'd shared with them.

Evolution was what happened
as the story of ecstatic wonderment
was passed through life
from ear to ear,
changing slightly
with each iteration.

She set truth to dancing
with the whirl of Her planets
and kissed the nucleus of everything
with her only real ordinance:

"Make your love visible."

ACKNOWLEDGEMENTS

This book was made possible by a small village, and the kindness of every contribution, large and small, permeates this text from start to finish.

My own experiences are but one wing that gave this book flight; the other is the heart of Chelan Harkin. Her willingness to shine her relentless light of Divine truth inspires me more than any words can convey.

Many of the events that helped me tell the story of our awakening journey have happened as a direct result of the love, support, friendship and inspirational mojo of Corene Crossin. I can't imagine this journey without her.

The look and feel of this book was made possible by Cheri Warren and Ashlee Eikelboom, who elevated my ideas for the cover and interior art from doodles on a napkin to wondrous storytelling imagery, and Isabell VanMerlin, who added her magic touch to the overall layout. Glenn Hovemann and Muffy Weaver provided wise guidance in selecting the title. Gina Denny, Judith Kern and Elliott Robertson provided editorial encouragement early in the process, and Lisa Dewey, Steve Huck and Corene Crossin all spent many hours of support with meticulous reviews.

Others whose influence and support brought this book to life include Jodi Christiansen, Susan Davis, Anne Denman, Andrew Donald, Janet Ehrler, Charles Feerick, Dottie Framant, Julie Grace, Dyanne Griffith, Heather Hart, Barbara Heffel, Jane Hobson, Glenn Jones, Cinthia Kane, Holly Kersis, Todd Kramer, Joanne Kunin, Carol Lawson, June Longway, Eileen Lunny, Margarita Marnik, Diane Ducret-Mork, Judith Ouelette, Heather Phillips, Dee Sasseen, Theresa Seiverd, Taylor Stannard, Jane Sterken, Christina Strutt, Judy Wallace, Barbara Willeford, and all other members of my private community past and present. My life is enhanced immensely by their company on this wondrous adventure.

Thanks also to Paul Selig, Rasha, and Alfred K. LaMotte for their inspiring influence on me and our awakening world. Their light makes me feel less alone in illuminating the beauty and awe of all that is underway in our mystical odyssey.

ABOUT MARY AND CHELAN

Mary Reed was a staunchly agnostic healthcare executive living in Washington, DC when she began venturing uncontrollably into mystical experiences in the company of Jesus, Buddha and angels. She finally surrendered her "normal" life and spent several years in a tiny nunnery in the Himalayas coming to terms with her unexpected abilities. Her profound experiences are both a road map and an invitation into the Divine wisdom we all hold within. Mary's work is a palpable transmission of Divine Love as evidenced in this text and in her first two books, *Unwitting Mystic* and *Divine New Being*. To learn more about Mary and her courses, events, and private community, visit lovemaryreed.com.

Chelan Harkin is the quintessential mystic poet of our modern times. A young, prolific wordsmith perpetually open to the eloquent flow of Divine verse, Chelan's solo works thus far include her books *Susceptible to Light* and *Let Us Dance! The Stumble and Whirl with the Beloved*, and collaborative works *Taste the Sky* with Rashani Réa, and *Bouquet of Stars* featuring twelve Poetry Chapel poets. To learn more about Chelan and her poetry visit chelanharkin.com.

Made in United States
Troutdale, OR
07/29/2024

21633420R00159